WAGES AND PROFITS IN THE CAPITALIST ECONOMY

NEW DIRECTIONS IN MODERN ECONOMICS
SERIES
Series Editor: Malcolm C. Sawyer, Professor of Economics, University of York

New Directions in Modern Economics presents a challenge to orthodox economic thinking. It focuses on new ideas emanating from radical traditions including post-Keynesian, Kaleckian, neo-Ricardian and Marxian. The books in the series do not adhere rigidly to any single school of thought but share in common an attempt to present a positive alternative to the conventional wisdom.

The main emphasis of the series is on the development and application of new ideas to current problems in economic theory and economic policy. It will include new original contributions to theory, overviews of work in the radical tradition and the evaluation of alternative economic policies. Some books will be monographs whilst others will be suitable for adoption as texts. The series will highlight theoretical and policy issues common to all modern economies and is designed to appeal to economists throughout the world regardless of their country of origin.

Published titles:

Post Keynesian Monetary Economics:
New Approaches to Financial Modelling
Edited by Philip Arestis

Keynes's Principle of Effective Demand
Edward J. Amadeo

New Directions in Post-Keynesian Economics
Edited by John Pheby

Theory and Policy in Political Economy:
Essays in Pricing, Distribution and Growth
Edited by Philip Arestis and Yiannis Kitromilides

Keynes's Third Alternative?
The Neo-Ricardian Keynesians and the Post Keynesians
Edward J. Amadeo and Amitava K. Dutt

WAGES AND PROFITS IN THE CAPITALIST ECONOMY

The Impact of Monopolistic Power
on Macroeconomic Performance
in the USA and UK

ANDREW HENLEY
Keynes College, University of Kent at Canterbury

Edward Elgar

Published by
Edward Elgar Publishing Limited
Gower House
Croft Road
Aldershot
Hants GU11 3HR
England

Edward Elgar Publishing Company
Old Post Road
Brookfield
Vermont 05036
USA

British Library Cataloguing in Publication Data

Henley, Andrew
Wages and profits in the capitalist economy: the impact of monopolistic power on macroeconomic performance in the USA and the UK. - (New directions in modern economics)
1. Capitalist countries. Income. Distribution
I. Title II. Series
339.2

ISBN 978 1 85278 090 6

Printed and bound by CPI Group (UK) Ltd, Croydon, CR0 4YY

Contents

Illustrations

Tables

To Sue and James

Author's note
Following common convention the term billion indicates thousand million.

Preface

The emergence of interest in what has come to be termed post-Kaleckian economics has brought with it concern for the issue of the importance of imperfectly competitive markets on the macroeconomy. This book aims to provide an applied economist's survey of developments in this field and to offer evidence to suggest that the implications of monopolistic power are of importance to an understanding of macroeconomic performance. This is done by focusing on the distribution of income between wages and profits, and on aggregate profitability in general. For some readers a focus on income distribution may seem strangely dated, yet the distribution of income was at the centre of Kalecki's analysis. And in the present author's opinion it is at the centre of any understanding of the observed pattern of aggregate profitability. Profitability is of crucial importance to functioning of the macroeconomy, influencing investment and therefore growth. The style of this book is not polemical, but rather it offers an appraisal, informed by evidence for both the USA and the UK, of these propositions. The origins of this book lie in my doctoral thesis (University of Warwick 1986). The origins of my interest in Kaleckian economics lie as a graduate student with the late John Brack, and subsequently with my doctoral supervisor Keith Cowling. I am also especially grateful for the help of Malcolm Sawyer as editor of the **New Directions in Modern Economics** series, and as one better qualified than most to comment on a work on Kaleckian economics. A number of colleagues at the University of Kent at Canterbury have, without implication, also commented on various sections of the book in its present and in earlier forms and have pointed my research in the right direction, particularly Steve Bazen, Alan Carruth, Richard Disney, Howard Gospel and Tony Thirlwall. Finally my thanks go to my wife Sue who, as one who practises at the 'sharp end' of social science, tries hard to inform my academic interests with a breath of the real world.

1. Introduction

Is the pattern in which income is divided between labour income and profits of importance to our understanding of the growth and development of the capitalist economy? As a general rule the orthodox Keynesian–neoclassical synthesis finds that it is not. Investment is modelled as a function of output, not of profits. The price level and the level of real wages are determined by demand, not by the extent of the profit mark-up. Both the Keynesian and Neoclassical models, at least as they appear in most textbooks, are built on the foundation of perfect competition in the product market and so aggregate underemployment of resources or aggregate price instability are explained by imperfections in the working of the labour market. This is paradoxical in view of the fact that as modern macroeconomic analysis was emerging in the 1930s so was the modern analysis of oligopoly and imperfect competition. This latter development has led to the vast postwar growth in the microeconomics of industrial organization, largely built on the premise of non-perfectly competitive markets. The Kaleckian tradition, by recognizing the difference between price and output determination under perfect competition and under oligopoly or monopoly, blends a Keynesian-style focus on aggregate demand determination with a Marxian-style concern for the division of income generated in the production process. So imperfections in product markets as well as imperfections in the labour market are of importance to an understanding of macroeconomic performance. Neoclassical and new-classical economists see macroeconomic performance as following entirely from the aggregation of microeconomic equilibria. Keynesian economics has, in response to the stagflation of the 1970s, belatedly started to address the relationship between microeconomics and macroeconomics. The Kaleckian approach has always addressed the importance of the microfoundations of macroeconomics.[1] In very simple terms the functional distribution of income is determined at the microeconomic level by the behaviour of oligopolistic firms, conditioned by the bargaining power of monopolistic trades unions. Functional distribution in turn affects macroeconomic performance because it affects profit rates and capacity utilization and therefore the investment plans of capitalists, and possibly also consumption. Because the profit mark-up or 'degree of monopoly' is conditioned by trade union bargaining, the political economy of wage determination enters the Kaleckian analysis as an important ingredient. The Kaleckian approach can be seen as providing a departure from, rather than a break with, conventional macroeconomic analysis (Fine and Murfin 1984), since it introduces a relaxation of the assumption of a perfectly competitive market structure. Very recently other approaches have also started to make the same departure, by focusing on the consequences of imperfect competition for relative adjustment of prices and output (Blanchard and Kiyotaki 1987). This work can be seen in terms of starting from the same point of departure but placing a different emphasis on the consequences of imperfect competition.

The question of the implications of a growing degree of monopolization both at the level of the domestic and the international economy is the concern of the 'monopoly capitalism' school.[2] The monopoly capitalism literature generally appeals to the work of Kalecki as a principal influence and particularly his 'degree of monopoly' theory of distribution, although its origins can be traced to the work of such Marxist writers as Lenin and Hilferding (Sawyer 1988). Auerbach and Skott (1988) identify two main themes found in this literature. The first is that historically the twentieth century has witnessed the emergence of large monopolistic corporations within developed capitalist economies, which have come to dominate many sectors of the economy. In more recent literature this is generally analysed using a model of profit-maximizing oligopolistic price and output determination (Cowling and Waterson 1976). The second is that this growth in monopoly power has generated a secular tendency towards macroeconomic stagnation. A third theme (Fine and Murfin 1984,

Cowling and Sugden 1987) is that more recently the growth of transnational corporations has led to monopolization of markets at the global level and therefore to global stagnation. At the static level Kalecki's asserted relationship between distribution and monopoly power may well be supported empirically. One aim of this book is to provide a survey of evidence for this. However one obvious criticism of the ideas of the monopoly capitalism school is that in recent years the longer established capitalist economies such as the UK and the USA have found themselves subjected to increasing levels of competition from more recently developed economies. In structural terms this means that markets within the UK and the USA appear less concentrated once account is taken of increased import penetration. Second, the stagnation of the 1920s and 1930s which provided the inspiration for the work of such authors as Kalecki and Steindl (1952) has not, at least until the 1980s, been repeated in the postwar period. Indeed most capitalist economies, of which the UK and USA provide no exception, enjoyed an unprecedented period of prosperity and economic growth during the 1950s and 1960s. The faltering of economic growth in the 1970s is generally attributed to the effect of energy price increases, macroeconomic mismanagement, growing trade union power and even growing international competition rather than to any growth in monopoly power. However the influence of monopolistic behaviour, and its interaction with the countervailing pressure of trade union behaviour, may be of importance to an understanding of the cyclical behaviour of the capitalist economy. A second aim of this book is therefore to provide a thorough descriptive analysis of the behaviour of the rate of profit and of distributive shares in the UK and US economies over the cycle and trend for the postwar period, drawing on the influential work of Weisskopf (1979).

A further very important theme in the work of Kalecki is his concern with the political economy of the relationship between government policy and policy formulation and capitalist development. This is perhaps most clearly typified by his paper 'Political Aspects of Full Employment' (Kalecki 1943). The ideas developed in this paper arguably spring from the notion that government macroeconomic policy will influence the functional distribution of income and profitability. That influence will in turn generate capitalist antipathy to interventionist policies. So a third aim is to provide an assessment of this for our understanding of the postwar performance of the UK and US economies. The rest of this introduction provides an overview of the remaining chapters of the book. Chapter 2 provides a brief review of orthodox theories of the functional distribution of income, concentrating principally on the neoclassical analysis of factor shares. The principal problems to have emerged with the neoclassical approach concern the realism of marginal productivity theory, which defines the relationship between factor employment and remuneration. Marginal productivity theory encounters considerable difficulties when translated to a world of oligopolistic price and output indeterminancy, and to a world characterized by bargaining between oligopolistic firms and trades unions. The Kaleckian degree of monopoly approach to the supply-side determination of income distribution is discussed, both in Kalecki's original conception and as extended in the light of modern developments in oligopoly theory. This complements a focus on technological considerations with one on the institutional and structural conditions holding within product markets. The Kaleckian approach is completed by a discussion of the determination of aggregate demand. The two sides of demand determination and cost conditions are brought together in the approach of Rowthorn (1981) to provide a simple model of the determination of profitability.

Chapter 3 concentrates on the question of the determination of the 'degree of monopoly' and points out the relationship with the industrial organization literature. In particular the relationship with two strands of this literature is discussed. The first strand is the concentration–profits issue and the second the question of the relationship between market structure and price formation. The chapter also reviews recent empirical tests of the degree of monopoly model of wage share, and reports some cross-section evidence for US manufacturing industries in 1972. It concludes, in the light of microeconomic evidence, by drawing some implications of oligopolistic structure for macroeconomic performance.

In Chapter 4 we concentrate on the influence of collective organization of workers on the determination of the degree of monopoly. First some theoretical considerations are discussed: the inadequacy of the perfectly competitive neoclassical approach, the contribution of recent developments in the microeconomic analysis of trades unions within the context of product market monopoly power and an extension of this to include Kaleckian mark-up pricing. The implications of this for the relationship between trade union bargaining strength and profitability are assessed and empirical evidence for this, and the relationship with wage share, are surveyed. As in the previous chapter, this chapter concludes with a discussion of recent work relating trade union behaviour to macroeconomic performance.

Chapters 5, 6 and 7 address the question of the determination of aggregate profitability. Chapter 5 reviews explanations for cyclical and secular movements in profitability. It then presents the profit rate decomposition methodology first used by Weisskopf (1979) in his analysis of profitability crisis in the non-financial corporate sector of the USA between 1949 and 1975. This shows how movements in capacity utilization, income distribution and capital productivity contribute to movements in the rate of profit, and in turn how movements in factor productivity and remuneration affect these three. The analysis is extended to allow further decomposition of labour share into production and non-production (or overhead) remuneration shares, and the share of income devoted to non-wage labour costs. Chapter 6 presents evidence using this decomposition for the USA from 1949 to 1985 and Chapter 7 evidence for the UK from 1962 to 1985. The approach used allows decomposition of movements in profitability over the intra-cyclical, cyclical and secular periods. The decomposition of labour share into various sub-components in turn allows a better assessment of the applicability of Kaleckian distribution theory to the secular time span of the postwar period.

Kalecki's concern with the relationship between aggregate profitability and the stimulation of aggregate demand through Keynesian-style policy interventionism has already been introduced. In Chapter 8 we discuss this more thoroughly, providing a reappraisal of Kalecki's ideas, and an assessment of their relevance to an understanding of the postwar performance of the US and UK economies. The chapter also speculates about current prospects, particularly in terms of the efficacy of alternative policies aimed at stimulating economic growth and alleviating unemployment. The conclusion drawn is that solutions may not be as straightforward as suggested by a more conventional Keynesian demand-management approach. Chapter 9 provides a brief concluding summary.

NOTES

1. Recent work on macroeconomics from a post-Kaleckian point of view include Sawyer (1982a, 1982b), Rowthorn (1981) and Reynolds (1987).
2. A non-exhaustive selection of the main contributions to the monopoly capitalism school includes Baran and Sweezy (1966), Cowling (1982), Foster and Szlajfer (1984), Dutt (1984), Cowling and Sugden (1987). Fine and Murfin (1984), Auerbach and Skott (1988) and Sawyer (1988) provides surveys and critiques.

2. Neoclassical Distribution Theory and the Kaleckian Alternative

The question of what determines the functional distribution of income is one that seems to have largely disappeared from the agenda of academic economists in recent years. In part this may be explained by the divergence between the theoretical properties of the neoclassical general equilibrium model and the empirical realities of the recent economic experience of the western capitalist nations. The properties are those of a world of perfect competition in which changes in factor distribution are governed largely by the technical conditions surrounding the way in which those factors are combined in the production process, since the pricing of those factors is determined by the forces of supply and demand in perfectly competitive factor markets. General equilibrium in such a world is characterized by full-employment Pareto-optimality, although uniqueness and stability of that equilibrium cannot be guaranteed (Arrow and Hahn 1971). Nevertheless Frank Hahn eloquently defends the usefulness of neoclassical general equilibrium approach as follows:

When the claim is made – and the claim is as old as Adam Smith – that a myriad of self-seeking agents left to themselves will lead to a coherent and efficient disposition of economic resources, Arrow and Debreu show what the world would have to look like if the claim is true. In doing this they provide the most potent avenue of falsification of claims... (Hahn, 1973, p. 14, quoted by Howard, 1979, p.63)

However this argument presupposes a negative role for neoclassical theory, effectively reducing it to the role of an economic theory for economic theorists to gauge their alternatives against, offering little or nothing in the way of predictive content

7

for analysis of the real world. Neoclassical growth theory[1] hence serves to highlight the conditions under which an economic system might achieve balanced full employment growth and the properties associated with that steady state but fails to predict and explain unbalanced growth in an imperfect economic system in which resources lie idle. And neoclassical distribution theory sheds no light on – indeed it assumes away – the political economy of how the fruits of economic growth are divided between competing recipients.

In addition to this, much of the debate surrounding distribution theory in the 1960s became weighed down in the seemingly unresolvable technical debate concerning the analytics of the use of an aggregate production function to represent the physical relationships between factors of production and the output of the economic system – the reswitching controversy.[2]

To return to our first point it is clear, in the present author's opinion, that one of the most important failings of the neoclassical model is its strict adherence to the assumption of perfect competition. Distribution theorists, and not exclusively those writing from within a strictly neoclassical framework,[3] seem to have largely ignored the influence of monopoly power, to the extent that the casual observer might be forgiven for thinking that the equality of price and marginal cost was some sacrosanct article of faith.

In attempting to draw together various heterogeneous strands of thinking on distribution theory Joan Robinson (1960) identifies several propositions essential, in her view, to a general theory of distribution. The first proposition is that, as suggested by the neoclassical model, relative factor shares are governed by factor supplies and the technical relationship existing between them in the production process. However, Robinson adds three further propositions which clearly lie outside the scope of the neoclassical model. The first of these is that factor shares are determined by the pricing policy of firms. It is not unreasonable to assume that the enjoyment by a firm of some degree of monopoly power in its product market gives it flexibility to allow its product price to rise above the perfectly competitive marginal cost level. If monopolistic power is a structural feature of an economy then that will have a bearing on relative factor shares. The second proposition is that 'relative shares are governed by the rate of investment and the propensity to consume of each class' (Robinson, 1960, p. 353). This proposition is the central feature of Kaldor's model and the determination of investment, coupled to the degree of monopoly, is, as we shall see, an important feature of Kalecki's theory. The final proposition is that 'the relative shares depend on the relative bargaining strength of workers and employers' (ibid., p. 354).

SUPPLY-SIDE EXPLANATIONS: NEOCLASSICAL THEORY

Many excellent surveys of neoclassical distribution theory exist elsewhere[4] and it is not the intention of the present author to attempt to reproduce, with probably considerably less success, that which other authors have already done. Traditional neoclassical analysis of factor shares is firmly rooted in the neoclassical theory of production. At the heart of this is the production function. To progress from a technical relationship between inputs and outputs one needs to be able to say something about the relationship between factor productivity and factor remuneration. The crucial link from neoclassical production function to income distribution is therefore marginal productivity theory.

In the context of a perfectly competitive model with two homogeneous and perfectly divisible factors (usually identified as 'labour' and 'capital') it can be shown that the trend of labour share will be determined by the elasticity of substitution between the two factors and the bias of technical progress.[5] Labour share will remain constant if the elasticity of substitution is equal to 1 and technical progress is 'Hicks-neutral'. In a world of capital-using technical progress a constant labour share over time would require that the elasticity of substitution was sufficiently less than 1 so that the drop in demand for labour relative to capital was exactly offset by the drop in the supply of labour relative to capital. This drop in relative labour supply is brought about by the effect of technical progress in increasing the relative size of the capital stock. Empirical analysis of the behaviour of factor shares in such a framework is therefore complex, largely because of difficulties in incorporating technical progress into an econometrically estimated production function. Technical progress requires that the econometrician distinguish between shifts along the production function from shifts in the function. In practice the modelling techniques used start from some *a priori* notion about the form of technical progress (usually that it is 'disembodied'), and so are *ad hoc*. It is also usually assumed to be exogenous and therefore determined by forces external to the production system. Cross-sectional studies, which are able to sidestep dynamic considerations, have generally found that the elasticity of substitution was for a broad array of industries in a number of economies and at varying points in time reasonably close to 1.[6] In their important seminal paper which introduced the constant elasticity of substitution production function Arrow *et al.* (1961) obtained values of the elasticity of substitution of between 0.7 and 1 for various manufacturing industries. If the hypothesis that the elasticity is insignificantly different from 1 is not rejected, that technology is of the standard Cobb–Douglas form. Overall, combining observable statistics indicating an upwardly trending labour share over the 50 years after the First World War[7] with econometric results supporting generally neutral technical progress[8] and an elasticity of substitution somewhere just below 1, the neoclassical framework is able to construct a reasonably consistent empirical story. However these results are not sufficient in themselves to offer proof for the neoclassical story, and to validate the use of the assumptions that it makes. The results may be quite consistent with other relationships. For example a point often made is that econometric results purporting to describe a particular technology may be simply describing a cost function.

Fundamentally two principal criticisms of the neoclassical approach to distribution have emerged,[9] both of which strike much further than the raising of problems associated with the econometric use of production functions. The first concerns the realism of marginal productivity theory (Thurow 1976, Kaldor 1966) and the second challenges the practical analytical use of marginal productivity theory as providing a link between technology and distribution as a result of the problem of reswitching, already alluded to. The condition that in equilibrium factor prices are set equal to the value of the output produced by the unit of the factor employed at the margin is, of course, derived from the first order conditions for profit maximization in a perfectly competitive firm. As Thurow points out:

To apply marginal productivity it is necessary to specify the extent to which the distribution of economic prizes is a marginal productivity distribution and the extent to which the distribution of economic prizes reflects monopolies. (Thurow 1976, p. 218)

There is no difficulty in providing a neoclassical theory of distribution under monopoly, which takes account of reduced derived factor demand under monopoly and equality of marginal revenue products rather than average revenue products with factor prices. However, as Thurow points out, most real world industrial structures lie between the polar extremes of monopoly and perfect competition. Price and output setting under oligopolistic conditions are characteristically indeterminate, governed by industrial structure and the extent to which behaviour is rivalrous or collusive.[10] A very clear illustration of this indeterminacy is provided by using the example of Sweezy's kinked demand curve model (Sweezy 1939). This model, because it generates a discontinuity in the firm's marginal revenue function, generates a range of factor price levels consistent with the marginal productivity equilibrium condition in the firm's factor markets. Hence changes in factor shares, perhaps resulting from increased labour bargaining power in the firm's labour market, could occur that would not involve any movement from the firm's equilibrium position on its production function. So we clearly see that relaxation of the assumption of a perfectly competitive product market in this case requires us to take account of the influences of industrial structure and of relative bargaining strengths of buyers and sellers of factors. We shall illustrate this more formally using a very simple oligopoly model shortly.

Certainly at the level of the aggregate economy to attempt to explain distributional patterns solely in terms of the parameters of a neoclassical production function with no reference to institutional conditions governing price and output setting in industrial markets entails the assumption that the economy can be characterized as competitive. Many industrial sectors of capitalist economies such as those of the UK and the USA are structurally far from atomistically competitive. Although structurally markets may depart significantly from the atomistic ideal modern industrial organization theory suggests that this need not imply any strong divergence from the competitive price and output benchmark levels.[11] Nevertheless the most recent evidence would suggest that monopoly power in the USA and the UK does involve sizeable resource misallocation. Cowling and Mueller (1978) estimate the static deadweight loss due to profit-maximizing monopoly resource misallocation to be just under 4 per cent of gross corporate product for both the UK and the USA, or in absolute terms over \$4.5 billion for the USA using data for the period 1963–66 and £385 million for the UK using data for the period 1968–69. Sawyer (1980), using UK industry data for 1963, obtains a static deadweight loss estimate of just under 7 per cent of national income. Such estimates ignore any allowance for the costs of obtaining and preserving a monopoly position (Posner 1975), costs which might include advertising expenditures and expenditure on investment in strategic entry-deterring excess capacity (Lyons 1986). Cowling and Mueller, when adding advertising expenditures and current super-normal profit,[12] suggest that the resource misallocation may be as high as 7.2 per cent of gross corporate product for the UK and 13.1 per cent for the USA.

The analytical problem of reswitching, which is a theoretical possibility in all but the simplest model with homogeneous factors of production or only one sector, undermines the existence of a precisely formulated aggregate relationship between technology and factor prices and hence between technology and distribution. In conjunction with Sraffa's (1960) critique of neoclassical production theory the reswitching controversy has served to show the impossibility of sustaining in aggregate a neoclassical explanation for the division of income between capital and labour income. Reswitching (or capital reversal) occurs when the same production technique (factor combination) is chosen at two different factor price ratios, though at factor price ratios in between a different technique is chosen. Hence a monotonic relationship between factor prices and technique does not exist. The problem arises in models with more than one sector because of difficulties in the aggregation and therefore the measurement of capital. Capital must be defined in value terms and that value will change as factor prices change (the Wicksell effect); hence it is not possible to provide an independent, consistent measure of factor intensity.[13] The reason why this problem has such devastating theoretical consequences for the aggregate use of marginal productivity theory and production function-based distribution theory is that it shows that more than one wage rate (or profit rate), and hence more than one distribution of income is consistent with any given production technique. Therefore the reswitching problem destroys any production function-based model of aggregate distribution. In a disaggregated form marginal productivity theory remains intact requiring that the marginal product of each item of capital (i.e. machine) is equated with its price. Since all but the most primitive forms of economic activity involve heterogeneous factors of production, for practical purposes where some degree of aggregation is necessary this critique undermines such models of distribution at virtually all levels. Analysis of distribution from a strictly non-neoclassical point of view must therefore utilize concepts of economic efficiency in terms of cost minimization rather than productive efficiency in the physical relationship between inputs and output (Hicks 1965, Craven 1979). Harcourt in his survey of the Cambridge capital debate states that:

(d)issatisfaction with or outright rejection of marginal productivity theory has been associated with a plea for a return to modes of analysis in which, if you like, pricing is an aspect of distribution rather than, as in neoclassical thought, distribution being but an aspect of pricing. (Harcourt 1972, p. 9)

He cites as responses to this plea neo-Keynesian macroeconomic theories of distribution and, *inter alia*, the pricing-based theoretical work of Kalecki.

The Keynesian school's dissatisfaction with the theoretical rigour of the neoclassical approach led to a complete change of focus from sole preoccupation with the supply side to sole preoccupation with the demand side. The principal development was that of the Kaldor–Pasinetti 'Keynesian' model of distribution (Kaldor 1955, Pasinetti 1962, 1974), which highlights the importance of relative savings propensities between capitalists and workers in determining relative income shares. In Kaldor's simplest formulation (1955) the determination of income is not modelled – it being assumed that income is at the full-employment level.

At given savings propensities capitalists' profit depends on how much they invest. As a theory of distribution it is of course incomplete since it contains no supply side to allow determination of the level of income and therefore assertion rather than explanation of relative savings propensities. However Kalecki (1971a) (originally published before Kaldor) closes his model of the capitalist economy with an aggregate demand equation incorporating differential savings propensities. We shall return to the 'Keynesian' model of distribution in our discussion of Kaleckian models of capitalist development.

SUPPLY-SIDE EXPLANATIONS: THE KALECKIAN ALTERNATIVE

The theory of income distribution developed by Kalecki represents an attempt at explaining microeconomic distribution from within a more realistic framework of imperfectly competitive mark-up pricing, which avoids all the aggregation problems associated with neoclassical production function-based theory. Although initially conceived as an explanation for distributional patterns during the stagnationary economic conditions experienced by capitalist economies during the 1930s, it can be thought of more generally as applying to those sectors of the capitalist economy in which, to use Kalecki's own phrase, prices are 'cost-determined'. At the core of the model is a short-run monopolistic mark-up pricing equation, the mark-up of price on prime cost being determined by what Kalecki termed the 'degree of monopoly'. For the individual firm Kalecki asserts that its price (p) is formulated according to the following rule:[14]

$$p = m u + n \bar{p} \tag{2.1}$$

implying that price is set by applying a mark-up (m) to unit prime cost (u) plus some proportion of average industry price ($\bar{p}$). The second term is included to capture the desire of firms to ensure that their prices do not become too high relative to those of rivals. So if a firm faces a cost increase it will increase its prices accordingly, but only by the same proportion as the cost increase if average industry prices rise proportionately. In other words the extent to which cost increases are passed on into prices will depend on whether rival firms simultaneously experience similar cost increases. Aggregating over all firms in the industry we obtain:

$$\bar{p} = (m / (1-n))\, u \qquad (2.2)$$

so $m/(1-n)$ captures the industry mark-up factor. Some authors[15] have confusingly understood this mark-up factor itself to be the 'degree of monopoly', but strictly speaking this view represents a misinterpretation of Kalecki's intention. He states:

The coefficients m and n characterising the price-fixing policy of the firm *reflect* what may be called the degree of monopoly of the firm's position.
(Kalecki 1971a, p. 45, emphasis added)

Equation 2.2 can be rewritten as:

$$\bar{p} = k\, u \qquad (2.3)$$

where k is the industry mark-up factor. If we multiply through by the level of output we obtain a relationship between total revenue and total prime costs:

$$\bar{p}\, Q = \Pi + O + W + M = k\, u\, Q = k\, (W + M) \qquad (2.4)$$

where Π is profits, O overhead costs, W wage costs and M materials costs. Rearranging we have:

$$\Pi + O = (k - 1)\, (W + M) \qquad (2.5)$$

Defining value added (Y) as $\Pi + O + W$ we can obtain the following expressions for profit and wage shares of value added at the industry level:

$$\frac{\Pi}{Y} = \frac{(k - 1)\, (j + 1)}{(k - 1)\, (j + 1) + 1} - \frac{O}{Y} \qquad (2.6)$$

$$\frac{W}{Y} = \frac{1}{(k - 1)\, (j + 1) + 1} \qquad (2.7)$$

here $j = M/W$, the ratio of materials costs to wages costs. So we obtain an inverse relationship between k (and hence the degree of monopoly) and wage share and a positive relationship between the degree of monopoly and profit share. Furthermore as overheads as a proportion of value added rise, *ceteris paribus*, profit share falls. We also obtain an inverse relationship between wage share and ratio of materials to wages cost, and a positive relationship between profit share and this ratio. Aggregating to the level of the whole economy Kalecki identifies the relative price of imported raw materials as representing the most important influence on j (Sawyer 1985a).

Neoclassicals and others were quick to criticize Kalecki, principally on the grounds that the theory is tautological.[16] Postwar textbooks on distribution theory have generally dismissed Kalecki's contribution in a couple of paragraphs, often describing it as 'unorthodox' with the implication that it does not warrant close consideration. It was obtained, it is generally argued, from a simple rearrangment of an identity and possesses no behavioural content. Consequently it is untestable since it does not relate the price–cost margin behaviourally to such variables as the bargaining power of workers or the prevalence of oligopolistic industrial structure (Reder 1959). But as already hinted this view seriously misunderstands Kalecki's ideas and condemns the intuition behind them rather than recognizing the limitations of his algebra. In fact an algebraic 'missing link' between the mark-up and the degree of monopoly was only provided by Cowling and Waterson (1976) almost 40 years after Kalecki's original paper. We shall discuss this link shortly. As Sawyer (1985a) points out, the absence of an explicit formulation of such a link in Kalecki's work does not mean that such a relationship does not exist. Indeed most of the empirical tradition of industrial economics of the last 35 years, from Bain (1951) onwards, has been largely grounded in the conceptual framework of establishing and analysing links between industrial performance and market structure and oligopolistic behaviour. The price–cost margin is one of the commonest used measures of industrial performance. Ferguson's objection to the degree of monopoly theory led him to the conclusion that it is empirically false (Ferguson 1969) since its predictions are derived from assumptions of constant unit cost and general excess capacity. This conclusion is unwarranted since constant unit cost is quite plausible in a world in which oligopolistic firms hold excess capacity for strategic entry-deterring purposes (Spence 1977, Dixit 1980). Furthermore, in arguing that the degree of monopoly theory is an unrealistic characterization of postwar US manufacturing industry, Ferguson fails to recognize that relaxation of the assumption of constant unit cost does not invalidate the idea of mark-up pricing. It merely makes the relationship between prices and costs more complicated. Kalecki justifies the use of this simplifying assumption by his observations of stagnationary economic conditions in the 1930s, conditions of market cartelization, declining capacity utilization and falling investment opportunities driven by a declining purchasing power of worker-consumers. Nevertheless Kalecki does not appear to have abandoned the idea that distribution is determined by the degree of monopoly, returning to the subject in his last published paper (Kalecki 1971b).

It is clear from careful reading of Kalecki's work that he believed that a behavioural relationship exists between the size of the monopolistic mark-up and the institutional nature of the environment in which a firm operates, although he did not make this link explicit in a mathematical sense. He identifies specifically two factors at work:

First and foremost the process of concentration in industry leading to the formation of giant corporations should be considered... Such a firm knows that its price p influences appreciably the average price p̄, and that moreover, the other firms will be pushed in the same direction because their price formation depends on the average price p̄. Thus the firm can fix its price at a higher level than would otherwise be the case. The same game is played by other big firms and thus the degree of monopoly increases substantially. (Kalecki 1971a, pp. 49–50)

He goes on to discuss how this process can lead to tacit collusive agreements and then to full-blown cartelization. The second factor is:

The development of sales promotion through advertising, selling agents, etc. Thus price competition is replaced by competition in advertising campaigns etc. These practices will obviously cause a rise in the degree of monopoly. (Kalecki 1971a, p. 50)

Working against the influences of concentration and advertising intensity Kalecki also considered that trade union bargaining power would in certain circumstances restrain the size of the degree of monopoly mark-up. We shall return to the question of the impact of trades unions in Chapter 4.

Kalecki's conception of the relationship between the price–cost margin and market structure would be regarded today as rather simplistic, although we must recognize that when he was originally writing, with the exception of work by Chamberlin (1933) and Robinson (1933) on imperfect competition, economists had made little progress in exploring price and output determination under oligopoly. He seems to relate the size of the mark-up within an industry to that industry's position on a degree of monopoly continuum from competition through collusion and cartelization to monopoly. In contemporary industrial capitalist economies explicit collusion is much less prevalent, especially in view of the enactment and use of much wider anti-trust legislation than existed before the Second World War. Despite this markets are on average more concentrated (Hannah 1983). So the link between the size of the mark-up and conditions of concentration and collusion is not so clear. Indeed oligopolistic market behaviour can be characterized as much by rivalrous behaviour as collusive behaviour.

A second difficulty with the degree of monopoly theory concerns the treatment of the income share of overhead labour.[17] This occurs due to the use of a short-run prime-cost mark-up in the pricing model which forms the basis of the theory as described here. Because of this Kalecki must distinguish between labour costs that in the short run may vary with the level of output and those that do not. Hence equation 2.7 provides only a determination of the share of direct wages. Kalecki does at one point remark that it would be of greater interest to consider the share of labour (direct and indirect) as a whole (Kalecki 1939, p. 13). However later in the same work he does seem to suggest that a distinction can be drawn between those salaried workers who are 'clerks' and those who are 'managers', the distinction being that changes in the salaries of white-collar clerical staff will be closely related to changes in manual wage rates, and that changes in managerial salaries will be related to changes in profits. Sawyer (1985a) points out that subsequent writers on Kaleckian distribution theory appear to have adopted one of two alternative approaches to the division of labour costs into variable and overhead labour costs. The first approach is based on a straight distinction between those costs that vary with output and those that do not within the relevant time period over which pricing decisions are formulated. This distinction hinges on an accurate definition of 'marginal cost'. As a quantity marginal costs in practice may be difficult to pin down, particularly if the extra costs of a future change in output are unknown. If, as may often be the case, firms announce prices in advance of production then their estimates of marginal cost used in those pricing decisions may turn out to be different from actual marginal costs. Hence some researchers on oligopolistic pricing have tended to make use of a concept of 'normalized' direct costs (Coutts *et al.* 1972).

The alternative approach hinges more on a sociological distinction between 'managers' and 'workers'. In the UK and the USA statistical conventions in official manufacturing industry censuses divide labour costs into costs of production workers (or 'operatives' in the UK) and the costs of non-production or 'administrative, technical and clerical' staff. Sawyer (1985a) argues that it is more difficult to reconcile these statistical conventions with this second approach. On the other hand other authors, in applied work (Phelps-Brown and Hart 1952, Cowling and Molho 1982), suggest that the divergence between overhead labour costs and 'managerial' salaries is not too great. Cowling (1982) sees the growing proportion of administrative, technical and clerical staffs in total employment as indicative of the rising overall importance of the managerial function, both as a means to increase control over technical and administrative aspects of managing production and in order to satisfy the desires of managers to be seen to be presiding over large staff departments.

To return to the problem of Kalecki's 'missing link' between the size of the mark-up and the degree of monopoly, we noted that a theoretical link has been derived by Cowling and Waterson (1976).[18] Starting from the basis of oligopolistic profit maximization the following expression for aggregate industry wage share of value added can be derived (see Appendix to the chapter for a full derivation):

$$\frac{W}{Y} = 1 - (\frac{H}{\epsilon}(1 + \mu)) \frac{R}{Y} \qquad (2.8)$$

where W/Y is wage share of value added, H the Herfindahl index of industrial concentration, ϵ the product elasticity of demand, μ is a weighted average of the firms' 'conjectural variation' terms capturing their perceived output setting interdependence (explained in fuller detail in the Appendix), and R/Y the ratio of sales revenue to value added.

Equation 2.8 shows an inverse relationship between wage share and the level of industrial concentration, and a positive relationship between wage share and the modulus of the elasticity of demand, so as product demand becomes more elastic the potential for raising price above average variable cost falls and so wage share rises. In the case of the average conjectural variation term μ equation 2.8 suggests that there is an inverse relationship between the 'degree of collusion' and wage share. *Ceteris paribus*, wage share will be highest where firms perceive no interdependency (the Cournot case) where $\mu = 0$. Wage share will be lowest in the other limiting case of collusion where firms determine output levels together as a joint monopolist.[19] The importance of the relative size of raw materials costs will be captured by R/Y. As in Kalecki's version there is a one-to-one inverse relationship, *ceteris paribus*, between profit share and the share of income devoted to overheads. Hence an increase in the size of managerial expenditure will cause a correspondingly direct fall in profit share. Furthermore if capacity utilization falls, output will fall but fixed costs will remain constant and hence profit share must fall.

Debate has arisen concerning the applicability of the degree of monopoly theory to the examination of long-run changes in income distribution in view of the underlying short-run pricing hypothesis.[20] In any short-term period wage share is determined by the degree of monopoly prevailing at that period. Kalecki held the view that 'the long run trend is but a slowly changing component of a chain of short period situations' (Kalecki 1971a, p. 165). Within each 'short period' only the labour input is variable. Factor proportionality may of course change over the long run and so we might expect shifts in the degree of monopoly through changes in the composition of costs. If we simplify the analysis to consider solely the Cournot oligopoly case and introduce a simple two-factor linearly homogeneous production technology (disregarding problems of capital aggregation), we can obtain the following expression for each firm's wage share of value added (again see the Appendix for derivation):

$$\frac{wL_i}{Y_i} = \frac{\epsilon - s_i}{\epsilon} - \frac{rK_i}{Y_i} \tag{2.9}$$

Once again the elasticity of demand, ϵ, and market structure (captured through firm i's market share, s_i) enter as determinants of wage share. Wage share for firm i is smaller the smaller its market share. Furthermore wage share falls as the share of capital costs rise, and in this case due to the assumption of linear homogeneity in technology on a one-for-one basis. So a change towards a more capital-intensive (in terms of cost) production technique will reduce wage share.

THE ROLE OF AGGREGATE DEMAND

The previous section has outlined supply-side considerations for the way in which a given product is distributed between wages and profits. We now proceed to complete the picture by investigating how that level of output is determined and then draw some implications for the macroeconomic behaviour of the capitalist economy. The previous section developed a model of profit generation under oligopolistic conditions. In this section we shall analyse the conditions which determine whether those profits are 'realized' and in very general terms the dynamic aspects of that process.

Kalecki himself combined a theory of differential savings propensities with the degree of monopoly theory to obtain a theory of the determination of the level of income. Kalecki regarded as self-evident the proposition that workers save proportionately less of their income than capitalists and generally assumed, for analytical convenience, that workers' saving was zero. This assumption generates for Kalecki the simple conclusion that gross capitalist profits must equal the sum of gross investment and capitalists' consumption, since the other component of aggregate demand, namely workers' consumption, exhausts wages and salaries. This leads to the well-known remark, attributed by Kaldor (1955) to Kalecki, that 'capitalists earn what they spend and workers spend what they earn'. For Kalecki the behavioural content in this simple manipulation of macroeconomic aggregates enters through his theory of the determination of investment. He saw current investment expenditure as determined by past investment decisions which in turn are largely governed by gross savings, the rate of change of aggregate profits and the rate of change of the capital stock.[21] Current savings can be seen as adjusting to meet capitalists' investment requirements. However for present purposes we do not need to develop discussion of the determinants of investment in any detail. We shall return to the question of the long-run behaviour of investment in the capitalist economy shortly. Following Sawyer (1985a), relaxing the zero workers' saving assumption, but simplifying initially to a closed no-government economy, we can combine the degree of monopoly and income determination in the following way. From equation 2.6 we can write:

$$\Pi/Y = d - O/Y \tag{2.10}$$

where d is a function of the degree of monopoly and the raw materials/wages ratio. Therefore:

$$\Pi = dY - O \tag{2.11}$$

Total income, if divided in income terms, is divided between wages, profits and overhead managerial labour payments and, if in expenditure terms, between consumption and investment. So:

$$Y \equiv \Pi + W + O \equiv \Pi + C_w + S_w + C_o + S_o$$

$$\equiv I + C_c + C_w + C_o$$

where C_w, C_c, C_o are consumption by workers, capitalists and managers and S_w and S_o are workers' and managers' savings.[22] Substituting into equation 2.11 we obtain:

$$dY + C_W + S_W = I + C_c + C_W + C_O \qquad 2.12$$

and rearranging we obtain the following expression for income:

$$Y = \frac{I + C_c + C_O - S_W}{d} \qquad (2.13)$$

Relaxing the assumption of a closed economy with no government equation 2.13 becomes:

$$Y = \frac{I + C_c + C_O - S_W + G - T + X - M}{d} \qquad (2.13a)$$

where G is government expenditure, T taxes, X exports and M imports. Equation 2.11 would now refer to post-tax profits and consumption and savings are post-tax magnitudes. Equation 2.11 shows that the volume of profits depends on the level of income which from equation 2.13a is governed by capitalist and managerial expenditure (consumption and investment), workers' savings, the degree of monopoly and the state of the government budget and balance of trade. So if capitalists are able to raise their degree of monopoly, profit share will rise but their volume of profits will remain unchanged. This is because the increase in the degree of monopoly, through d, will have a correspondingly negative effect on the level of income. Hence capitalists may enjoy the potential to create a greater volume of profits, through an increased degree of monopoly but will, *ceteris paribus*, be frustrated in their attempts to realize those profits.

The idea of differential savings ratios is incorporated by later writers, particularly Kaldor and Pasinetti, into their neo-Keynesian theories of distribution. These models rest on an assumption of full employment and so lack the generality of Kalecki's theory in which the level of income can be restrained below full employment by monopoly influence. Kaldor's well known model (Kaldor 1955) proceeds from the assumption that planned investment is equal to planned savings. Profit and wage shares depend on relative savings propensities (and crucially for sensible results that $s_W < s_c$) and the investment–income ratio. With fixed propensities the crucial determinant of distribution is solely investment.

Kalecki himself held the opinion that the level of investment generated by the capitalist economy would in the long run be insufficient to maintain a full-employment level of income. To achieve the maintenance of full employment by stimulation of private investment would require cumulatively increasing efforts to offset the influence of a falling rate of profit (Kalecki 1945). He cites the need for a steady exogenous stream of innovation for the continual rejuvenation of the level of attractiveness of further investment projects (Kalecki 1954, Chap. 15). Furthermore he argues that capitalists inherently strive towards a higher and higher degree of monopoly through the concentration process. One likely consequence of this, implied by equation 2.13, is a declining rate of growth of real output. Steindl (1952, 1979) develops this idea into a theory of capitalist stagnation in which rising concentration leads to rising unplanned excess capacity which in turn reduces further the attractiveness of new investment, leading to increasing difficulties in profit realization. Oligopolists respond, according to Steindl, to declining effective demand by making output reductions rather than price reductions and so capacity utilization continues to fall.[23] So the process goes on until some exogenous factor restores the level of effective demand or rejuvenates the attractiveness of investment. Declining capacity utilization also places downward pressure on potential profit through its effect on the relative size of overhead costs (as implied by equation 2.6).

The relationship between profits and capacity utilization is illustrated very clearly in a model developed by Rowthorn (1981), which encapsulates the ideas of Kalecki and Steindl. Rowthorn derives a two-equation model of profit determination with one equation providing the relationship between realizable profit and capacity utilization (the 'profits curve') and the other the relationship between potential profit and capacity utilization (the 'realization curve'). Actual profits and capacity utilization are determined by the joint solution of the two. We shall derive a largely similar model here. Potential profit is determined by the degree of monopoly, but is conditioned by the relative importance of overhead costs. Overheads are assumed to be proportional to the level of capacity output, Y^*, so $O = \alpha Y^*$. Equation 2.11 can therefore be re-expressed as:

$$\Pi = dY - \alpha Y^* \tag{2.14}$$

We define capacity utilization, u, as Y/Y^*. We will assume that capacity output is determined by the size of the capital stock, K, so $Y^* = \sigma K$. Equation 2.14 can therefore be rearranged to obtain the following expression for the rate of profit:

$$\Pi/K = \sigma du - \sigma \alpha \tag{2.15}$$

Equation 2.15 is the 'profits curve'. The potential rate of profit rises as capacity utilization and the degree of monopoly, reflected by d, rises and falls as the overhead burden rises. Realizable profit is determined by aggregate demand. We will assume for simplicity zero savings from labour income, so:

$$S = s_c \Pi \tag{2.16}$$

The rate of investment (I/K) is assumed to be determined in a simple linear fashion by the current profit rate and the state of capacity utilization. So we have the following investment function:

$$I/K = i_0 + i_1(\Pi/K) + i_2 u \tag{2.17}$$

The standard income–aggregate demand equality condition for an open economy with a government requires that:

$$S = I + G - T + X - M$$

Combining this with equations 2.16 and 2.17 we have:

$$s_c \Pi = (i_0 + i_1(\Pi/K) + i_2 u)K + G - T + X - M \tag{2.18}$$

Further manipulation yields the following expression for the rate of profit:

$$\frac{\Pi}{K} = \frac{i_2 u}{s_c - i_1} + \frac{G - T + X - M}{K(s_c - i_1)} + \frac{i_0}{s - i_1} \tag{2.19}$$

– the 'realization curve'. So, *ceteris paribus*, the realizable rate of profit will rise as capacity utilization rises. Equations 2.15 and 2.19 therefore jointly determine the rate of profit. Figure 2.1 illustrates diagrammatically the two equations. It can be easily demonstrated that for levels of output below the capacity level stability requires that the 'profits curve' be steeper than the 'realization curve' (see Rowthorn 1981).[24]

Rate of profit

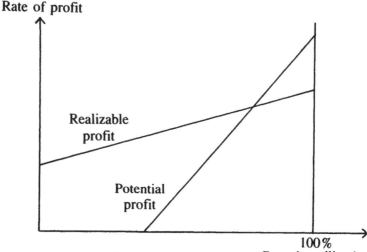

100%
Capacity utilization

Figure 2.1   Potential and realizable profit

Figure 2.1 serves to provide a focus on the importance of various factors for capitalist macroeconomic performance. First Kalecki's proposition that capitalist development requires a steady flow of innovation to rejuvenate investment attractiveness suggests that left to their own devices capitalists' investment behaviour will be characterized by a steady decline in the i_0 parameter of the investment function. This will cause the realization curve to shift downwards leading to lower capacity utilization and the rate of profit. Innovation is required to maintain the position of the realization curve. Second, an increase in the degree of monopoly shifts the profits curve upwards with the result that both capacity utilization and the rate of profit decline, because the associated output reduction reduces effective demand and so worsens the conditions governing the realization of profit. So Kalecki's proposition that 'the degree of monopoly has undoubtably a tendency to increase in the long run because of the process of concentration' (Kalecki 1938, p. 109) means that the dynamic behaviour of capitalism will, in the model presented here, be *ceteris paribus* characterized by a declining profit rate and a declining level of capacity utilization. Hence, as Bleaney (1976) points out, it is sometimes argued that the Kaleckian framework is an underconsumptionist one in the sense that maldistribution of income, through an increased degree of monopoly, leads to declining effective consumer demand. However, strictly speaking it is inadequate investment, and not declining consumer demand, caused by declining capacity utilization that determines the reduced effective demand, though we might expect consumer demand to fall if wage share falls. McDonald (1985) assesses the implications for variations in the price-cost mark-up in the Kaldor–Mirrlees growth model. In a similar manner a rising mark-up leads to declining investment and aggregate demand deficiency. Auerbach and Skott (1988) point out that the Rowthorn result that an increasing degree of monopoly leads to a declining profit rate and capacity utilization rate hinges on the specification of the investment function. They detail a variation of the model arguing that in the long run investment is highly sensitive to the rate of capacity utilization, and obtain a 'knife-edge' result that in steady state the warranted growth rate is characterized by a positive relationship between the degree of monopoly and the rate of profit. This issue of the long-run sensitivity of investment to changes in capacity utilization is an empirical one, and the point made by Auerbach and Skott does not rule out short- and medium-term stagnationary effects of an increase in the degree of monopoly.

Third, this simple model clearly shows that if a rising degree of monopoly characterizes the 'natural' dynamic state of the capitalist system then profitability crisis can only be averted through the appearance of some externally generated upward movement in the realization curve. Kalecki's 'innovation factors' might be one such source of this. There are others. Rosa Luxembourg (1963) argues the need for the capitalist economy to generate 'external markets' in order to maintain effective demand and avoid realization crisis and in a late essay [25] Kalecki agrees with this though he rejects the argument that the capitalist system must depend solely on effective demand generated from overseas sources to survive. In effect he extends Luxembourg's definition of external markets to cover not only net trade outflows from non-capitalist (or strictly speaking non-monopoly capitalist) sectors but also demand generated through the government budget deficit. In particular he focuses on the effect of war and armaments expenditure on profit realization, citing the then contemporary effect of the Vietnam War on the US economy.[26] The role of the government budget deficit in providing a means for the realization of 'potential surplus' is extensively analysed by Baran and Sweezy (1966) who point to the imporance of growing expenditure on both civilian government and militarism in maintaining the level of effective demand in the twentieth century US economy. However there is some confusion in Baran and Sweezy's work concerning whether it is the size of the government deficit or the absolute size of government expenditures themselves that is important. If it is the latter then the rejuvenative effect must come through the effect that this has on the investment function through reduced capacity utilization (Bleaney 1976). Baran and Sweezy also suggest that wasteful expenditures by large corporations have helped prevent crisis. This is reflected through an increased propensity to consume on the part of capitalists and in Baran and Sweezy's view particularly consumption of a managerial discretionary nature. Monopoly capitalist corporations in contemporary economies, they argue, also devote enormous resources into sales effort aimed at generating and restimulating demand for production. Related to this Brack and Cowling (1983) suggest that advertising has been successful in creating wants among American consumers during the twentieth century by finding evidence that advertising has induced an outward shift in workers' labour supply curves. In addition a number of studies which incorporate advertising into an aggregate consumption function have found that consumption is raised by advertising (Taylor and Weiserbs 1972, Peel 1975, Metwally and Tamaschke 1981).

Kalecki draws one further point of importance concerning capitalist development in a well known paper 'Political Aspects of Full Employment' written in 1943 (Kalecki 1971a, Chap. 12). In it he expresses doubt about the ability and the desire of the *laissez-faire* capitalist system to maintain full employment. He points out that capitalists' attitude to reflationary public expenditure and investment is schizophrenic. Initially they are keen to encourage the state in generating business 'confidence' through the creation of new government contracts and through the beneficial effect on aggregate demand of government transfers. However Kalecki argues that it is fallacious to suppose that capitalists will desire prolonged attempts at maintaining full employment since the dynamics of the capitalist economy require larger and larger government deficits to do this. He suggested a number of reasons why they will object to a prolonged period of rising budget deficits, and therefore why the macroeconomy might be characterized by a 'political–business' cycle. We shall return to this in Chapter 8.

In particular he points out that under a regime of continued aggregate demand-stimulating deficits, social and political changes would undermine the social position of employers in that the threat of redundancy would cease to be effective and the bargaining power of workers would become intolerably strong. This, of course, is a common theme whether in the Marxist guise of the dwindling of the 'reserve army' or in the guise of the orthodox Phillips curve relationship.

APPENDIX

The Cowling–Waterson link between profitability and concentration

The Cowling–Waterson (1976) model starts from a framework of oligopolistic profit maximization using an individual firm profit function for firm i that captures that firm's conjectures concerning rivals' (firms j) output responses to a change in firm i's own output:

$$\Pi_i = p(Q)q_i - C_i(q_i) - F_i \qquad i = 1 \ldots n \qquad (A2.1)$$

where Q is the industry output, q_i is the output of firm i, $C_i(.)$ is firm i's total variable cost function and F_i is firm i's fixed costs. Maximization of profit requires the following first and second order conditions be satisfied:

$$\frac{d\Pi_i}{dq_i} = p + q_i \frac{dp}{dQ} \frac{dQ}{dq_i} - C_i' = 0 \tag{A2.2}$$

and

$$\frac{d^2\Pi_i}{dq^2_i} < 0$$

The term dQ/dq_i in the first order condition captures the oligopolistic interdependency – the conjectured effect of firm i's output on the other firms' outputs. Defining Q_j as Σq_j, for all $j \neq i$, we can express dQ/dq_i as $1 + \tau_i$ where $\tau_i = dQ_j/dq_i$. τ_i is therefore firm i's 'conjectural variation term' capturing its perceived output interdependence.[27] Equation A2.2 can be rearranged to give the following expression for firm i's price–marginal cost margin:

$$\frac{p - C'_i}{p} = \frac{s_i(1 + \tau_i)}{\epsilon} \tag{A2.3}$$

where $s_i = q_i/Q$, the output share of firm i and ϵ is the modulus of the industry elasticity of demand. We can sum across all i firms in the industry by returning to equation A2.1 and aggregating, making an assumption that marginal cost equals average variable cost. So:

$$\Pi + F = \overset{i}{\underset{n}{\Sigma}} p(Q)q_i - \overset{i}{\underset{n}{\Sigma}} q_i C'(q_i) \tag{A2.4}$$

If we divide the right-hand side of equation A2.4 by pQ ($= R$) we obtain the industry price–cost margin which is equal to the right-hand side of equation A2.3 aggregated across all firms:

$$\frac{\Pi + F}{R} = \frac{\overset{i}{\underset{n}{\Sigma}} p(Q)q_i - \overset{i}{\underset{n}{\Sigma}} q_i C'_i(q_i)}{pQ} = \frac{\overset{i}{\underset{n}{\Sigma}} s_i^2 (1 + \tau_i)}{\epsilon} \tag{A2.5}$$

So the industry ratio of profits plus fixed costs (i.e. the gross margin) to revenue is:

$$\frac{\Pi + F}{R} = \frac{H}{\epsilon}(1 + \mu) \tag{A2.6}$$

where $H = \Sigma s_i^2$ and is the Herfindahl index of concentration and $\mu = (\Sigma s_i^2 \tau_i)/\Sigma s_i^2$ and is a weighted average of each firm's conjectural variation term. Defining wage share as the share of direct wages (W) in value added (Y) so that $Y = \Pi + F + W$, we can therefore easily obtain the following expression for wage share of value added:

$$\frac{W}{Y} = (\frac{H}{\epsilon}(1 + \mu))\frac{R}{Y} \tag{A2.7}$$

Wage share in a Cournot oligopoly with variable factor proportions

If we combine the first order condition for profit maximization (equation A2.2) with a simple production technology[28] we can, for illustrative purposes, isolate the influence of the composition of cost from changes in factor proportionality on wage share. We will assume for tractability, that firms have Cournot conjectures. The first order condition for profit maximization reduces to:

$$p + q_i \frac{dp}{dQ} = C_i(q_i) \tag{A2.8}$$

This is the familiar condition that marginal revenue equals marginal cost. Marginal revenue for a non-perfectly competitive firm is governed by the slope of the industry demand curve (dP/dQ) and the scale of the firm's output (q_i). We will assume that that output is determined according to a two-factor linearly homogeneous technology of the form $q_i = f(K_i, L_i)$ where K_i and L_i are firm i's capital and labour input. The assumption of linear homogeneity allows us, using Euler's Theorem, to express (A2.8) as:

$$p + \left[\frac{\delta q_i}{\delta L_i} L_i + \frac{\delta q_i}{\delta K_i} K_i \right] \frac{dp}{dQ} = C_i^t(q_i) \tag{A2.9}$$

Now marginal cost $C'_i(.)$ will include marginal capital costs. Introducing the condition that marginal products will be set equal to factor prices over marginal revenue we can write:

$$p + \left[\frac{wL_i}{p + q_i \, (dp/dQ)} + \frac{rK_i}{p + q_i \, (dp/dQ)} \right] \frac{dp}{dQ} = C'_i \, (q_i) \tag{A2.10}$$

Multiplying through by q_i and rearranging we obtain:

$$pq_i - C'_i(q_i)q_i = \frac{s_i}{\epsilon - si} \, (wL_i + rK_i) \tag{A2.11}$$

Dividing by firm i's revenue, pq_i, we then obtain the following expression for firm i's price–cost margin, and on the assumption of constant unit variable costs, its ratio of profits + (non-capital) fixed costs to revenue:

$$\frac{\Pi_i + F_i}{R_i} = \frac{pq_i - C_i^t(q_i)q_i}{pq_i} = \frac{s_i}{R_i(\epsilon + s_i)} \, (wL_i + rK_i) \tag{A2.12}$$

Since unit variable cost now includes unit capital costs the following definition holds:

$$\frac{\Pi_i + F_i}{R_i} \left[\frac{R_i}{Y_i} \right] = 1 - \left[\frac{wL_i}{Y_i} + \frac{rK_i}{Y_i} \right] \tag{A2.13}$$

Further manipulation provides the following expression for wage share of value added:

$$\frac{wL_i}{Y_i} = \frac{\epsilon - s_i}{\epsilon} - \frac{rK_i}{Y_i} \tag{A2.14}$$

NOTES

1. For surveys see Solow (1970) and Dixit (1976).
2. Surveys of this debate are provided by Bliss (1975) and Harcourt (1972).
3. For example Kaldor's 'Keynesian' theory (Kaldor 1955) assumes price-taking behaviour.
4. Surveys of neoclassical distribution theory are provided by Ferguson (1969), Johnson (1973), and Howard (1979).
5. This result is established in Ferguson (1969, pp. 240–41).
6. An extensive survey of the large number of econometric production function studies of the 1960s is provided by Nerlove (1967).
7. See Feinstein (1968) for evidence of the trend of labour share in the UK and Kravis (1959, 1968) for evidence for the USA.
8. A comprehensive survey of the problems of dealing with technical progress is Kennedy and Thirlwall (1972).
9. With a wave of the (invisible?) hand we shall assume that the reader has no difficulties in suspending disbelief in perfect knowledge, factor divisibility, rationality on the part of economic agents, and absence of economic activity out of equilibrium.
10. For a good systematic survey of models of oligopoly highlighting the range of possible oligopolistic product market equilibrium solutions see Waterson (1984).
11. In particular recent ideas on the 'contestability' of markets suggest that the crucial link between monopolistic structure and non-competitive performance is to be found in entry conditions and that monopolistic structure need not imply resource misallocation (Baumol, Panzar and Willig 1983). However this view rests on highly restrictive assumptions about the nature of entry and cost conditions facing would-be entrants which seem to be lacking in robustness. More generally the 'Austrian' school of industrial organization would similarly regard high profits in the absence of artificially erected entry barriers as stimulating entrepreneurial activity towards competition, rendering monopoly profits as a temporary phenomenon (Littlechild 1981, Reekie 1979).
12. Posner (1975) argues that any would-be monopolist would invest in creating a monopoly to the point where those investment costs equal discounted expected future supernormal. Therefore the annualized cost of monopolization can be proxied by current supernormal profit.
13. Neoclassical authors have suggested schemes for overcoming this aggregation problem but they tend to rely on attempts to develop a 'quasi-homogeneous' concept of capital that limits the generality of the model. See Samuelson (1962), Levhari (1965) and Harcourt's review (1972).
14. The exposition here follows Kalecki's 1954 version of the degree of monopoly theory, reproduced as Chap. 5 of Kalecki (1971a). Basile and Salvadori (1984) and Kriesler (1987, 1988) provide a discussion of Kalecki's various expositions of his pricing theory.

15. One example is Kaldor (1955). Kalecki's use of the phrase 'degree of monopoly' has been discussed in a number of papers in the *Journal of Post-Keynesian Economics*, for example Reynolds (1983) and Basile and Salvadori (1984).
16. The tautology criticism of Kalecki's theory of distribution is made by, among others, Bauer (1944), Kaldor (1955), and Ferguson (1969).
17. The treatment of the income share of overhead labour is highlighted by, *inter alia*, King and Regan (1976).
18. For a more complete treatment of theoretical aspects of the profits-concentration relationship see Waterson (1984, Chap. 2).
19. In the Cournot case the gross margin to revenue ratio becomes H/ϵ and wage share equals $1 - (H/\epsilon)(R/Y)$. In the collusive monopoly case the gross margin to revenue ratio collapses to $1/\epsilon$ which is the familiar Marshall-Lerner index. Wage share in this latter case is equal to $1 - (R / \epsilon Y)$.
20. Riach (1971) and Askimakopulos (1975) both argue that in the long run firms would see their objectives in terms of the rate of return on capital, which might be inconsistent with the degree of monopoly. However, as Reynolds (1983) points out, Kalecki's degree of monopoly is the outcome of exogenous environmental and institutional factors and is not intended to serve as a corporate objective.
21. See Kalecki (1971, Chap. 10). Kalecki's ideas on investment are extensively discussed in Sawyer (1985a), and also in the wider context of post-Keynesian literature in Reynolds (1987).
22. This assumes that workers and managers receive no profit income from their savings.
23. This stagnationary process is analysed formally in the model presented by Dutt (1984).
24. In the present case this places the following lower bound on capitalists saving propensity:

$$s_C > i_l + i_0/(\sigma d)$$

25. 'The Problem of Effective Demand with Tugan-Baranovski and Rosa Luxembourg', Kalecki (1971a, Chap 13).
26. This is also discussed by Kalecki in a paper entitled 'Vietnam and Big Business', Kalecki (1972, pp. 107–114).
27. Different theories of oligopoly can be viewed as different theories of τ_i (see Waterson 1984). For example the Cournot case of extreme myopic behaviour is where $\tau_i = 0$ for all firms in the industry.
28. We will heroically ignore here the analytical difficulties concerning marginal productivity theory discussed earlier.

3. The Implications of Market Structure

The first aim of this chapter is to provide a review of three broad strands of empirical literature which follow from some of the theoretical issues raised in the previous chapter. First (and briefly) we shall investigate similarities between the predictions of the degree of monopoly theory and the empirical conclusions of the mainstream industrial organization literature. The second strand is closely connected in that it concerns oligopolistic industrial price flexibility, relating the way in which industrial prices are determined by conditions of market structure, particularly focusing on the question of whether prices tend to be demand- or supply-determined, and how that relationship might be conditioned by market structure. As we have seen in Chapter 2 the Kaleckian model of distribution has as its basis a supply-determined model of industrial price formation. The third strand, which will be covered in most depth, examines functional income distribution and market power. Empirical results on the relationship between wage share and concentration for a cross-section of US manufacturing industries are presented.

The conclusions to be drawn from this body of work are, generally speaking, that where markets are more monopolized profitability is higher, prices less sensitive to changes in demand conditions, cost changes are absorbed more easily through the price mark-up, and the distribution of the product swings in favour of profits and away from wage income. The final section of the chapter discusses the relationship between market structure and macroeconomic activity, illustrating the importance of market structure in understanding macroeconomic behaviour, as a prelude to examining distributional patterns in the aggregate economy.

CONCENTRATION AND PROFITABILITY

The orthodox industrial organization literature stemming from the seminal work of Bain in the 1950s (Bain 1951) has established very conclusively the existence of a relationship between industrial concentration and profitability. It is hardly the place here to begin to review this vast literature – surveys can be found in any modern industrial organization text (Sawyer 1985b, Clarke 1985) and exhaustive, though less up-to-date, surveys have been provided by Weiss (1974) and Bobel (1978). It suffices to point out that cross-sectional profits–concentration relationships have been established using a variety of differing measures of profitability and concentration for most industrialized economies using data for numerous points in time in the postwar period. Much further debate has focused on why this relationship occurs. However such studies have rarely, if ever, spelt out the distributional implications of this seemingly very robust relationship. These implications are very clear given the close relationship between the share of profits in income and orthodox measures of profitability, the profit rate and profit revenue ratio (or price–cost margin).

For the purposes of relating distribution to market structure we should in particular focus attention on those studies which employ a price–cost margin measure of profitability, since as shown in the previous chapter, wage share, profit share and the price–cost margin are closely linked definitionally. Generally speaking American researchers have traditionally preferred to model profit rates though more recently have presented results using both variables, whereas in the UK studies tend to adopt a price–cost margin of profitability.[1] The theoretical work of Cowling and Waterson (1976), discussed in the previous chapter, suggests that in fact the price–cost margin is the more appropriate dependent variable. As shown earlier in equation A2.6 in the formulation presented in Waterson (1984) we can derive the following result:

$$\frac{\Pi + F}{R} = \frac{H}{\epsilon} (1 + \mu) \qquad (3.1)$$

This result suggests that if we are interested in testing a relationship between profitability, as captured by the left-hand side of the equation, and industrial structure, as captured by H, the Herfindahl index of concentration, then the appropriate dependent variable should be defined as the ratio of profits plus overheads to revenue. The correspondence between profit rate and price–cost margin (or profit mark-up) will depend on the level of capacity utilization and capital productivity. In a cross-sectional sample of industries at a discrete point in time the effect of inter-industry variations in capacity utilization may be significant, hence explaining why very similar results have been obtained whichever measure of profitability has been used. Nevertheless Auerbach and Skott (1988) criticize the implicitly exogenous treatment of demand considerations within this conventional approach.

However a number of provisos need to be made before deducing distributional implications from the positive price–cost margin concentration relationship. This arises because the profit revenue ratio and the price–direct cost ratio are not necessarily equivalent. First, it is necessary to assume that marginal and average costs are the same; in other words that marginal cost is constant. This was demonstrated in the Appendix to Chapter 2. Second, we need to assume that profit is defined as a gross margin of revenue over direct costs, in other words that we are treating overheads as 'profit' for distributional purposes.

Cowling (1982) appeals to the literature on strategic entry deterrence (Spence 1977, Dixit 1980) as justification for the assumption of constant unit cost. In simple terms this literature argues that excess capacity can under certain circumstances act as a credible deterrent to potential competition, and so leads to the suggestion that oligopolistic industries will, if entry deterrence is being actively pursued, be characterized by conditions of excess capacity. Empirical evidence for the use of excess capacity for entry deterrence is sparse. Using data on 26 industries in the USA for the late 1950s Masson and Shannan (1986) find that where excess capacity is present it does indeed reduce rates of entry. However the level of capacity utilization does not appear to be set deliberately and strategically by oligopolistic firms in order to deter entry. Smiley (1988), from a recent questionnaire survey of 293 US companies, finds some evidence for the occasional use of excess capacity as a weapon of deterrence. However only 6 per cent of his sample admit to its frequent use.

The issue of whether it is appropriate to include fixed costs as an element of 'profit' is also contentious. Cowling (1982) argues that in so far as overheads include remuneration to overhead labour it is appropriate to treat these costs as being paid out of profit since, as discussed earlier, such staff might be presumed to identify with profit recipients. Empirical work such as Cowling and Waterson (1976) using the profit–revenue ratio and defining profit to include fixed costs presumably cannot rule out the possibility that concentration and profitability, so defined, are positively related for reasons other than the conventional explanation that more concentrated industries generate higher income. This is because we might expect them to carry a proportionately larger burden of fixed costs, perhaps because they experience poorer levels of capacity utilization. Nevertheless the relationship between profitability and concentration does seem robust to variation in the definition of profitability, be it defined as 'gross capitalist share' or as a more orthodox gross margin measure.

A further issue that arises in the empirical implementation of the Cowling and Waterson model concerns the empirical specification of the determinants of the aggregate conjectural variation term (μ) and the industry elasticity of demand (ϵ). μ is defined as a weighted average of individual firm conjectures, each weight being the firm in question's market share (q_i/Q). Fine and Murfin (1984) criticize this choice of weights on the grounds of the inappropriateness of the assumption of identical cost functions across different firms in the industry. Given that Cowling and Waterson make this assumption then it is correct that each firm's contribution to the industry degree of monopoly should be proportional to its contribution to the total restriction of output in the industry below the competitive level. If we relax the restrictive assumption of identical costs then we need also, Fine and Murfin argue, to take account of cost differences between firms in contributing towards the industry degree of monopoly and so the weights should reflect this.

Hence the intuition of Fine and Murfin's point is that μ as defined by Cowling and Waterson reflects only the effect of demand considerations on the degree of collusion. Presumably, they argue, if firms found themselves experiencing differing cost conditions they would wish to collude to achieve cost minimization. This point is important because empirical work cannot directly observe, and aggregate, individual firms' conjectural elasticities. In inter-industry empirical work researchers tend to sidestep the measurement of the conjectural variation term by either of two means. Cowling and Waterson themselves use time-differenced data and assume that across industries changes in μ between one year and the next are constant, hence not only assuming away inter-industry differences in the rate of change of collusion but also ignoring any inter-industry differences in changes in cost structures. Alternative studies assume that the degree of collusion is monotonically related to concentration across industries and so the effect of μ on profitability will be captured by the Herfindahl index. In the latter case this implicitly assumes individual firms' contribution to average industry collusion is weighted on the basis of market shares and so only reflects demand-side considerations. Other critics of the Kaleckian approach, especially those with a more orthodox Marxist point of view, argue that patterns of increasing concentration do not indicate reduced competitiveness. Auerbach and Skott (1988) argue that it is inappropriate to assume that geographical markets, or 'domains of competitiveness', have remained constant in size over time. The appropriate definition of markets is, of course, an issue that has always taxed empirical research in industrial organization.

The elasticity of demand is also unmeasureable. Again the researcher can, as Cowling and Waterson do, regress industry changes in profitability on industry changes in concentration and assume no inter-industry variation in the change in demand elasticity. Alternatively the industry elasticity of demand can be proxied. In their study on wage share, which we shall examine more closely later, Cowling and Molho (1982) propose the use of advertising intensity as a proxy, on the grounds that advertising serves to create buyer allegiance and so a more price-inelastic demand.

Reynolds (1984) examines the relationship between the degree of monopoly mark-up (defined as the ratio of sales revenue to materials and direct labour costs), concentration and other industrial structure variables as an explicit test of Kalecki's degree of monopoly theory of distribution. His data consist of a cross-section sample of 30 UK minimum list heading industries, where the combined market share of the five largest firms in each industry is above 80 per cent, for 1963, 1968 and 1977. His results are very mixed, the coefficients on the five-firm concentration ratio (CR5) being rather unstable with respect to changes in model specification and estimation procedure. For example a typical result for 1977 is the following:

$$\text{Mark-up} = 8.29 + 0.16 \ [\text{CR5}] - 0.00041 \ [\text{CR5}]^2 +$$
$$\quad\quad\quad\quad (2.51) \quad\quad (-1.6)$$

$$0.12 \ [\text{advertising intensity}] - 0.12 \ [\text{minimum efficient scale}]$$
$$(1.86) \quad\quad\quad\quad\quad\quad (-1.78)$$

$$+ \ \text{other variables} \quad\quad\quad\quad (t\text{-values in parentheses})$$

obtained using two-stage least squares estimation to allow for simultaneous determination of the mark-up and concentration. In Reynold's own words he concludes that the evidence concerning the effect of industrial concentration is suggestive rather than conclusive (Reynolds 1984, p. 79) of support for the degree of monopoly theory. However he, probably rightly, attributes this to poor data.

The conclusions one draws from the profits–concentration literature depends very much on one's interpretation of this seemingly robust statistical relationship. The alternative ideas concerning why profits and concentration are correlated have been well rehearsed elsewhere (Ferguson 1988, Clarke *et al.* 1984). The traditional structure–conduct–performance approach of industrial organization has generally interpreted this result as indicative of market power. The principal alternative explanation is the 'efficiency' hypothesis of Demsetz (1973) which argues that higher profits in more concentrated industries indicate greater efficiency, brought about through the cost advantage of being big. As Sawyer (1988) points out the monopoly capitalism literature comes firmly down on the side of the market power hypothesis.

INDUSTRIAL PRICING AND CONCENTRATION

This second strand of empirical literature provides some considerable justification for the model of price formation underlying Kaleckian theories of distribution. Specifically two broad issues have been addressed in the literature.[2] First, researchers have been concerned with the question of whether prices are sensitive to shifts in demand or are largely determined through a cost-based mark-up. The second issue concerns the question of the effect of market structure on industrial pricing. The two issues are closely related in that we would expect pricing to be much more sensitive to, and to adjust more quickly to demand changes under structures nearer to the perfectly competitive benchmark, and that the cyclical flexibility of prices may be less where concentration is high and competitive forces weak. Under more concentrated structures we might expect firms to attempt to collude in order to maintain mark-ups in the face of changes in unit costs. Hence changes in prices might closely reflect changes in cost conditions. On the other hand we might expect a similar close relationship to exist under more atomistic structures since competitive pressure would ensure that any changes in cost conditions become reflected in prices. Two methodological approaches seemed to have been adopted. The first is to examine the relationship between cost changes and price changes and to see if this relationship is dependent on the level of concentration across industries. The second is to specify or estimate some measure of price flexibility for each of a group of industries (in the case of Domberger 1979, a partial adjustment coefficient) and regress this measure on concentration in a cross-section.

The conclusion to be drawn from studies examining the relationship between price changes and cost changes is not clear. Three American studies (Ripley and Segal 1973, Lustgarten 1975, and Williams, Wilder and Singh 1977) conclude that more concentrated industries pass a smaller proportion of unit cost changes onto price changes. On the other hand De Rosa and Goldstein (1982) find no relationship between concentration and the proportion of cost changes passed on to price changes, but do find that prices are sensitive to demand shifts but that this sensitivity is greater where concentration is higher. Lustgarten

(1975) found that observed demand sensitivity was unrelated to concentration. Brack (1987) attributes this variety of results to the differing time periods over which price and cost changes are measured. He argues that true relationships will only emerge from a study of long-run price behaviour. Brack concludes from his own results looking at price changes over the period 1958–1970 for 390 four-digit US industries that more concentrated industries do in fact pass on less of their cost shifts, and that prices in concentrated industries are more demand-sensitive. More recent work for the USA has addressed the issue of differences in the cyclical behaviour of the price–cost relationship between concentrated and non-concentrated industries (Domowitz *et al.* 1986a, 1988, Rotemberg and Saloner 1986). We shall discuss these in greater detail in a later section of this chapter.

Results on the cyclical behaviour of pricing in oligopolistic sectors in the UK have been obtained that show that in such sectors prices are largely insensitive to changes in demand conditions. Godley and Nordhaus (1972) and Coutts, Godley and Nordhaus (1978) derive a 'normalized' measure of cost purged of the effects of changing labour input and productivity across the business cycle. They find that a predicted price obtained by applying a mark-up to this 'normal' cost predicts actual prices well across seven broad industry groups suggesting that demand influences on price are not important. Sawyer (1983) estimates a model for each of 43 UK industries to explain price changes and finds that in most cases changes are explained by changes in actual costs, and largely unrelated to demand pressures. He also estimates a cross-sectional model across 40 industries relating the change in prices over three cyclical downturns and two upturns to a quadratic function of the Herfindahl index. Limited support is found for the 'administered' price thesis that prices are less flexible in more concentrated sectors. Domberger (1979, 1983) estimates time series partial adjustment models of price formation, in which prices adjust to a desired level governed by cost levels and the state of demand, to obtain speed of adjustment coefficients for 21 UK industries. These adjustment coefficients are then regressed in a cross-section against various concentration definitions and it is found that prices adjust more quickly as concentration rises. Evidence therefore on the role of market structure in affecting the nature of price formation would appear to be very mixed.

Market structure is a notoriously difficult concept to capture statistically. The absence of reliable disaggregated time series data on concentration, particularly for the UK, make it very difficult to capture both dimensions of dynamic adjustment and market structure in a single econometric model. Furthermore oligopolistic pricing theory[3] suggests that pricing behaviour may well be conditioned by perceived oligopolistic interdependency, and as already pointed out in our review of the profits–concentration literature simple one-dimensional structural parameters (such as a concentration measure) may well fail adequately to capture the complex behavioural influences on price formation.

Henley (1988a) sidesteps the problems of an appropriate cross-section specification of the way in which price formation changes as concentration varies. This is done by estimating a dynamic time series model of price formation, albeit for a rather atypical example, namely the interwar British coal industry. Legislation in 1930 in this industry established regional cartels, and so there occurred a discrete transition from a competitive structure to an oligopolistic one. By estimating models separately for the 1920s and 1930s, controlling for demand and cost influences, it is found that cartelization across the British coalfields accounts for on average a 12 per cent increase in the mark-up. Furthermore after 1930 the speed of price adjustment to changes in costs becomes considerably slower.

What implications can we draw for distribution? There would be seen to be generally speaking broad support for a cost-plus based theory of pricing, along the lines of that at the basis of Kaleckian theories of distribution. On the other hand, but of rather less empirical significance to the relevance of the Kaleckian approach, the evidence on the relationship between cost-based pricing and market structure is mixed. This is further borne out by the mixed evidence on the speed at which firms in more concentrated industries adjust prices in response to cost changes. It is clear that results are very sensitive to prevailing macroeconomic conditions. We shall return to this point in a later section.

WAGE SHARE AND THE DEGREE OF MONOPOLY

The Kaleckian degree of monopoly theory of distribution focuses on the proposition that income shares are governed by the pricing policy of firms. The evidence from studies on industrial pricing supports the proposition that prices in oligopolistic sectors are largely determined by costs. Furthermore we have already seen that the size of the price cost margin is closely, and in a positive direction, related to market concentration. This evidence therefore leads to the suggestion that, at least in a static cross-section, income shares will be related to market structure, and specifically, wage share will be lower where concentration is greater.

An early study addressing the relationship between wage share and concentration was that of Moroney and Allen (1969). They looked at the impact of regional concentration on production worker wage share of value added across American manufacturing industries by regressing one against the other as a test of Kalecki's distribution theory. They find that concentration is not statistically significantly related to wage share and reject Kalecki's theory. However this is not surprising given the way in which the authors tackle the problem. They run separate regressions for each of 37 industries across US regions, hence implicitly assuming that each industry's market is regional in character and that regional concentration is important. Results suggesting support for the Kaleckian hypothesis are reported in an unpublished thesis by Barbee (1974). He regresses labour's share of value added on the four-firm concentration ratio and a capital intensity variable using data for 400 four-digit US manufacturing industries for 1963 and 1967. The coefficient on concentration carries a negative and well-determined coefficient.

More recent evidence for the UK is provided by Cowling and Molho (1982), from a sample of 118 minimum list heading industries for 1968 and 1973. Their dependent variable is the share of wages of production labour in value added (W/Y). Determinants of the degree of monopoly are captured through industrial concentration, measured as either the Herfindahl index (H) or the five-firm concentration ratio (CR5), and the ratio of advertising to sales revenue (A). They also include a measure of import penetration (IMP) to allow for the impact of international competition on domestic industrial structure and the investment–output ratio (I/Y) to control for the effect of differences in capital intensity across industries. Finally, included as a possible determinant of wage share is a measure of union power (U). We shall discuss more fully the relationship between distribution and trades unionism in Chapter 4. Cowling and Molho's results show a clear and robust negative relationship between their degree of monopoly variables and wage share. For example for 1968 they obtain:

$$\log(W/Y) = -2.902 - \underset{(-4.78)}{0.150} \log(H) - \underset{(-4.50)}{0.144} \log(A) +$$

$$\underset{(0.05)}{0.001} \log(IMP) + \underset{(1.54)}{0.144} \log(U) - \underset{(-1.42)}{0.079} \log(I/Y)$$

$$R^2 : 0.347$$

The figures in parentheses are t-statistics. The same model was estimated with salary share of value added as the dependent variable. A positive relationship is found between concentration and salary share indicating that as monopoly power increases some of the redistribution from wage share is paid to overhead labour rather than swelling profit share.

Cowling and Molho's work for the UK has been extended and updated by Conyon (1988). Conyon estimates a version of the Cowling–Molho estimating equation using pooled UK cross-section data for 1980 to 1984 and generally supports their conclusion of a significant negative relationship between the five-firm concentration ratio and production worker wage share. In particular Conyon finds strongest support for various non-linear formulations of the concentration–wage share relationship.

In a reply to Cowling and Molho, Brush and Crane (1984) attempt to show that a similar model estimated for a cross-section of manufacturing industries in the USA using data for 1967 does not support the degree of monopoly theory. They obtain poorly determined and even wrongly signed coefficients on their concentration measure. In a further reply Henley (1986a) raises a number of problems with the Brush and Crane results and reworks them, finding results much more akin to those of Cowling and Molho.

WAGE SHARE AND THE DEGREE OF MONOPOLY – FURTHER RESULTS FOR US MANUFACTURING INDUSTRY

In this section we present further cross-sectional results of a model relating wage share to determinants of the degree of monopoly using cross-sectional data for two manufacturing industry samples at differing levels of disaggregation.[4] Initially we adopt a single equation estimation model similar to that of Cowling and Molho (1982):

$$W/Y_i = \alpha_0 + \alpha_1 CR_i + \alpha_2 A_i + \alpha_3 KI_i + \alpha_4 U_i + \epsilon_i \tag{3.2}$$

The variables are as before, the only addition being a measure of capital intensity (KI). The i subscript refers to industry i. As a parameterization of the theoretical model derived to show the relationship between concentration and wage share (equations 2.8 and 2.9 of the previous chapter) this equation is an approximation to a precisely defined functional form, and so we must be careful in how we estimate it. Cowling and Molho (1982) prefer to report only results in a log-linear form, although clearly both linear or log-linear forms do not represent an exact formulation. On the basis of theory we expect negative signs on coefficients α_1, α_2, and α_3. If trade union activity is able to exert a counteracting influence on the size of the degree of monopoly mark-up then α_4 will carry a positive coefficient.

Our principal data source is the 1972 United States Census of Manufactures. 1972 is a fortunate choice of year since it gives us a cross-section just before the OPEC oil price increase that played havoc with the materials cost structure of western manufacturing industries. However our choice of observational unit was constrained by the problem that our unionization series is only available at the three-digit level rather than the more disaggregated four-digit level. Because of this we present results for a three-digit sample, including the unionization variable but using concentration data aggregated from the four-digit level. But in addition to provide more rigorous evidence on the concentration wage share relationship, by avoiding the difficulty of arbitrarily averaging four-digit concentration data to obtain a three-digit series, we include results for a larger four-digit sample of industries, but excluding the unionization variable. This four-digit sample, in order to ensure consistency in the results shown, is made up of the 215 four-digit industries which comprise the 71 three-digit industries in our three-digit sample.[5]

The concentration measure used is a four-firm concentration ratio (*CR*) compiled by Weiss and Pascoe (1981) for 1972.[6] To match the series to the three-digit database four-digit ratios were aggregated up using the proportion of value of shipments accounted for by each four-digit industry in the corresponding three-digit industry as weights. Advertising intensity is measured by the advertising sales ratio (*A*), derived in a similar fashion from the four-digit ratios of Ornstein (1977). Ornstein's data in fact refer to 1967 but are the only available at a sufficient degree of disaggregation. Furthermore they do not cover the full sample of industries. As a result our potential sample is reduced by around 30. The capital intensity variable used is a measure of the capital–labour ratio – the ratio of the 1972 book value of assets to production man-hours (*KI*). The unionization series used are those of Freeman and Medoff (1979) and measure the percentage of production workers (*UNP*) or percentage of all workers (*UNT*), depending on which dependent variable is being used, covered by a collective bargaining agreement. They refer to an average for the period 1967 to 1972.

We have already seen that because of the nature of the short-run pricing model at the core of Kalecki's theory, we must distinguish between labour costs that in the short run may vary with the level of output and those that do not. This distinction hinges on the definition of 'marginal cost'. In practice marginal costs may be difficult to pin down, particularly if the extra costs of a future change in output are unknown, or not known with certainty. The US Census of Manufactures allows us to distinguish between production and non-production labour costs. It might well be the case that some proportion of non-production labour costs is variable with the level of output, and conversely that a proportion of production labour costs is invariant, particularly if the production work-force in a firm embodies a significant degree of firm-specific human capital. For econometric purposes we are largely limited to noting this problem. However in the estimations presented here we use three alternative definitions of labour share, ranging from a narrow definition of production worker wage share to the broadest measure of the share of total labour costs, including employer payments to social insurance schemes (supplemental labour costs). The three measures used are:

WS1: Production worker payroll/value added

WS2: Total payroll (production workers and non-production staff)/value added

WS3: Total employee compensation (total payroll plus supplemental labour costs)/value added

In all three cases the denominator is value added in manufacture. These three measures are used to cater for differing opinions of who constitutes the employed class – from those who would argue that salaried staffs tend to identify with the managerial interest and that their share relative to profits is an *ex post* distributional issue between ownership interests and managerial interests to the orthodox viewpoint interested in the distinction between 'property income' and 'remunerative income'. If the narrowest definition (WS1) conforms most closely to direct labour costs then we might expect to find a stronger relationship between concentration and WS1 than with WS2 and WS3.

Table 3.1 presents ordinary least squares regression results for both logarithmic and levels specifications of the single equation estimating model (equation 3.2) using the three-digit database for all three definitions of the dependent variable.[7] Breusch–Pagan statistics indicate the presence of heteroscedasticity in the log specifications for WS2 and WS3, and so heteroscedastic-consistent *t*-statistics are reported. Heteroscedasticity is also present in the

Table 3.1 Ordinary least squares results for three-digit US cross-section 1972

Dependent Variable	Levels			Logarithms		
	WS1	WS2	WS3	WS1	WS2	WS3
Constant	0.368	0.537	0.591	−0.977	−0.863	−0.808
	(12.5)	(19.1)	(18.0)	(−3.79)	(−5.39)	(−5.06)
CR	−0.165	−0.101	−0.084	−0.093	−0.012	0.008
	(−4.58)	(−2.06)	(−1.46)	(−1.48)	(−0.31)	(0.20)
A	−1.430	−2.111	−2.434	−0.139	−0.124	−0.124
	(−4.87)	(−4.31)	(−4.24)	(−4.87)	(−4.78)	(−4.76)
KL	−0.002	−0.004	−0.004	−0.229	−0.204	−0.194
	(−3.75)	(−5.52)	(−5.33)	(−6.03)	(−7.44)	(−7.02)
UNP	0.085			0.172		
	(2.43)			(2.54)		
UNT		0.072	0.101		0.078	0.093
		(1.70)	(2.06)		(1.90)	(2.26)
n	71	71	71	71	71	71
$F(4,66)$	14.6	24.7	22.7	22.4	31.5	27.2
R-squared	0.470	0.599	0.579	0.576	0.642	0.622
BP $\text{chi}^2(4)$	1.67	4.18	6.24	3.42	13.25	13.78

Notes:

T-statistics, in parantheses, computed from heteroscedastic standard errors (White 1980).

$F(4,66)$ is a F-text for the joint significance of all the variables excluding the constant.

BP: Breusch–Pagan test statistic for heteroscedasticity (Breusch and Pagan 1980).

four-digit results presented in Table 3.2 and the same corrected *t*-statistics are reported there. First of all we should note the performance of our two product market structure and conduct variables – the concentration ratio and the advertising sales ratio. In all cases the advertising sales ratio carries a very well determined negative coefficient. From the logarithmic estimations we can note that a 10 per cent proportional rise in the advertising sales ratio is associated with between a 1.2 and a 1.4 per cent proportional fall in labour share. If we can assume that an increase in advertising

Table 3.2   Ordinary least squares results for four-digit US cross-section 1972

Dependent variable	Levels			Logarithms		
	WS1	WS2	WS3	WS1	WS2	WS3
Constant	0.384	0.555	0.618	−0.684	−0.375	−0.330
	(28.2)	(39.0)	(37.1)	(−5.62)	(−4.12)	(−3.59)
CR	−0.070	−0.067	−0.040	−0.019	−0.013	0.005
	(−2.04)	(−1.65)	(−0.83)	(−0.55)	(−0.50)	(0.19)
A	−0.011	−0.016	−0.018	−0.153	−0.132	−0.135
	(−6.26)	(−7.07)	(−6.94)	(−8.24)	(−8.53)	(−8.56)
KI	−0.002	−0.003	−0.004	−0.232	−0.190	−0.178
	(−5.81)	(−7.39)	(−7.09)	(−8.44)	(−9.25)	(−8.38)
n	215	215	215	215	215	215
$F(3,211)$	25.9	41.4	35.8	52.5	64.9	58.0
R-squared	0.269	0.371	0.337	0.427	0.480	0.452
LogL	231.4	212.1	178.3	−35.1	25.4	21.9
BP chi^2(3)	6.29	21.25	29.02	46.35	49.20	47.04

Notes: see Table 3.1

intensity is indicative of the strengthening of the power of firms in a monopolistic industry then we can see that this effect would have a clear impact on income distribution in that industry. The results for concentration are not as robust in terms of the levels of significance of the coefficients but nevertheless a negative association with the narrowest definition of labour share is reasonably well established.[8] This is confirmed by the four-digit cross-section results for the levels specification using the narrowest measure of labour share (Table 3.2). Various non-linear formulations of the relationship between labour share and concentration, as suggested by Conyon (1988), were also estimated. However, unlike for the UK, we found no evidence to suggest that a non-linear or non-log-linear specification improved the fit of the model.

We should note concerning the size of the coefficient on concentration that it decreases in size in all cases as the measure of labour income in labour share broadens, and becomes less statistically significant as the measure of wage share is broadened. We can conclude from this that there is a stronger inverse relationship between concentration and production worker payroll share than between concentration and the income share of white-collar staffs. This is further supported by the following two regressions with salary share of value added as the dependent variable:

Levels:
$$SS = 0.188 + 0.059\,CR - 0.791\,A - 0.001\,KI - 0.068\,UNT$$
$$(8.52) \quad (1.43) \quad (-3.18) \quad (-3.92) \quad (-2.27)$$

Heteroscedastic-consistent t-statistics in parentheses

$F(4,66)$: 5.25 R^2: 0.241 Logl: 115.3 BP (chi^2(4)): 9.16

Logarithms:
$$SS = -2.626 + 0.114\,CR - 0.102\,A - 0.179\,KI - 0.176\,UNT$$
$$(-6.29) \quad (1.09) \quad (-1.76) \quad (-3.24) \quad (-1.74)$$

$F(4,66)$: 3.55 R^2: 0.177 Logl: -29.8 BP (chi^2(4)): 3.83

Here we have a positive but not statistically significant relationship between salary share and concentration. Cowling and Molho (1982) also observed this for the UK. Their explanation was:

(I)n a world of managerial capitalism we would expect the size and expense of the salariat to grow with concentration as the managerial hierarchy skim off for themselves at least a fraction of the increment in profits and thus we would expect to observe a positive association with concentration. (Cowling and Molho 1982, p.101)

This result is quite consistent with the existence of profit-related bonus schemes for managerial employees. Turning back to the wage share estimations, the strongest results for unionization are obtained with production worker payroll share as the dependent variable. The logarithmic results indicate that a 10 per cent increase in the collective agreement coverage of production workers is associated with a 1.7 to 1.8 per cent increase in labour share. Using a wider definition of wage share and union coverage the effect is slightly smaller. So although not as robust in terms of statistical significance as for advertising intensity, we can note that a positive relationship is established for all three definitions of labour share. We can conclude from this that the impact of unionism is to mitigate the power of monopolistic elements in the product market in the determination of income distribution. Capital intensity is generally significantly negatively related to wage share.

These results address the question of what influence, if any, does monopolistic power in both product markets and labour markets of manufacturing industry have on income distribution, in the context of a cross-section of three-digit US industries. They provide evidence to support the view that the structure and market conduct of firms within an industry bear an important relationship to the functional distribution of income within that industry. Both concentration and advertising intensity have been observed to be negatively related to the share of value added going to production workers' wages. Advertising intensity continues to be significantly negatively related to labour share as the measure is broadened to include the remuneration of overhead labour. However the relationship with industrial structure is weakened considerably in this case. In the context of the discussion in Chapter 2 this indicates that, in addition to focusing on technological considerations, any explanation of income distribution must take serious account of the important influence of product market power. Also we have found a distinct positive relationship between labour share and the proportion of the appropriate workforce within an industry who are covered by a collective bargaining agreement. This suggests that the power of monopolistic firms to determine income distribution is at least partially offset by the impact of trades unions and collective employee organization. We shall discuss the implications of this last result in further detail in Chapter 4.

IMPLICATIONS FOR MACROECONOMIC PERFORMANCE

Monopolistic pricing was seen by Kalecki as generating very important implications for macroeconomic performance. The same importance is also attached to monopolistic pricing by subsequent writers developing work within a similar framework, such as Steindl (1952). As has been shown in Chapter 2 profitability enters such models as a crucial determinant of investment and therefore economic growth. More recent work, in a broadly neo-Keynesian tradition, has begun to incorporate imperfectly competitive product markets and therefore price-setting behaviour. These models demonstrate that monopolistic behaviour may lead to considerable sustained deviation from full employment macroeconomic equilibrium in the face of aggregate demand shocks. The impetus for theoretical developments in this area has come from growing dissatisfaction with the fundamental, yet unexplained, assumption of nominal price rigidity within the disequilibrium Keynesian approach of Clower (1965) and Leijonhuvfud (1968) and subsequent authors. Work has therefore focused on explanations for and implications of both real and nominal rigidity in both labour and goods markets. In the labour market research has followed a number of diverse routes such as job search and implicit contract explanations for unemployment (Frank 1986). Theoretical work on the macroeconomic implications of monopoly power in goods markets has focused on the costs of changing prices. Producers may face 'menu costs', and so price behaviour may become state-dependent, that is, only occurring if changes in demand are sufficiently large, or have accumulated sufficiently to outweigh these costs.⁹ In an imperfectly competitive world costs of price changes may need only to be small, since firms will typically carry excess capacity and so the costs of output adjustments will be low relative to price adjustment. Rotemberg and Saloner (1986) propose a model in which the degree of oligopolistic collusion is sensitive to movements in aggregate demand. They argue that in times of high demand oligopolistic industries tend to have relatively low prices. This is because in an oligopolistic industry where price might be the decision variable the benefits of undercutting price for a single firm are larger when demand is high. This result hinges on the assumption that punishment by other colluding firms will follow with a time lag, by which time demand will have fallen and the costs of punishment reduced. Hence price wars are more prevalent in booms. The length of the time lag between a price cut by one firm and response by rivals is an empirical issue. In aggregate terms Rotemberg (1982) observes that in the USA the price level is very sluggish to adjust to aggregate demand conditions. At a more disaggregated level Rotemberg and Saloner report a higher likelihood of a positive correlation between the real product wage (a measure of the price–cost margin) and output in more concentrated sectors of manufacturing industry. Hence in comparison with a competitive economy the dynamic behaviour of an economy characterized by substantial elements of price setting may be subject to considerable fluctuations in aggregate demand and to nominal price inertia. Blanchard (1987) finds evidence for the USA of substantial inertia in the adjustment of the aggregate price level to changes in input prices. However at the disaggregated level adjustment is quicker and he concludes that the cumulation of small lags in price adjustment leads to considerable sluggishness at the aggregate level.

Hall (1986) makes the point very strongly that macroeconomic fluctuations in the US economy reveal a good deal about market structure, and that the latter may be of great importance in the transmission of macroeconomic shocks. This, as has already been suggested, is because under conditions of 'chronic' excess capacity the trade-off between product price and output has few implications for overall profitability and so Hall concludes 'the incentives are weak for those business actions that would restore full employment'

(Hall 1986, p. 288). By reworking Solow's classic work on productivity growth (Solow 1957) Hall suggests that the observed procyclical movement in productivity for many sectors of the US economy boils down to non-competitive behaviour.

Nominal price inertia in a non-competitive economy has very strong implications for the behaviour of price–cost margins and hence for distributive shares over time. The important study of Sherman (1968) showed that profit margins in many US industrial sectors display substantial cyclical movement. This is confirmed by Hall's recent work (*op. cit.*), and also by work by Bils (1987). Bils finds across 21 US manufacturing sectors between 1956 and 1983 that if demand growth leads to a 10 per cent increase in the employment of production workers there will be in the short run an increase in marginal cost of 2.4 per cent, but a 3.3 per cent reduction in the price–marginal cost margin. Subsequent work by Domowitz, Hubbard and Petersen (1986a, 1988) investigates at a more disaggregated level the relationships between aggregate demand, profit margins and industrial concentration. In particular they find evidence that margins are more cyclical in more concentrated industries. This supports the idea of Rotemberg and Saloner (1986) about the greater prevalence of price cutting during booms. However they find evidence to question Hall's suggestion that high profit margins imply the existence of excess capacity. Over the period 1958 to 1981 they find evidence (Domowitz *et al.* 1986a) of a dramatic narrowing of the spread between margins in concentrated industries and those in less concentrated industries. Their results suggest that this is largely attributable to the greater sensitivity of margins in concentrated industries to aggregate demand fluctuations. The increasing international competition faced particularly by producers in more concentrated industries offers an additional though quantitatively less important explanation for this trend. This evidence is generally incompatible with a Keynesian world of nominal wage rigidity since most of the cyclical variation in price–cost margins comes about as a result of variations in cost. It is also incompatible with a world of competitive general equilibrium which would predict cyclically constant zero price–cost margins.

The recent developments discussed above clearly represent a considerable improvement on the traditional perfectly competitive basis to orthodox macroeconomic analysis, both of a Keynesian and neoclassical persuasion. Although the question of the cyclical behaviour of prices and profit margins in a non-competitive world has been addressed, and comparison has been drawn between dynamic behaviour in competitive and non-competitive sectors, little attention has been paid to the potential effect of changes in industrial structure on macroeconomic performance. This may in part be due to the paucity of time series information on movements in industrial structure, and the potential inadequacy of available measures of structure to capture 'market power'. The traditional view of Steindl (1952) is that in times of falling aggregate demand collusion will become more difficult to sustain and price wars more likely. This position is also the orthodox one to be found in the industrial organization literature (Scherer 1980). The converse is the analysis of Rotemberg and Saloner (1986). Cowling (1983) argues for greater collusion in slumps. Examining pricing behaviour during the severe recession in the UK of 1980–1981, he judges that the response to a downward demand shock will be an eventual increase in oligopolistic collusion, maintaining and possibly increasing profit margins. Econometric evidence for Norway (Berg 1986) supports the view that margins recover during an extended period of falling capacity utilization but not sufficiently to counteract the initial fall. Theoretical work by Sawyer (1982a, 1982b) has attempted to marry the Cowling and Waterson (1976) model of oligopolistic price and output determination with simple Keynesian and monetarist aggregate demand analysis, in order to demonstrate the importance of product markets as well as labour markets in the supply-side determination of output. The way non-competitive producers react to the price–output trade-off they face becomes crucial to equilibrium output and prices in the economy. The point that rising market power through its effect on the oligopolistic equilibrium price–cost margin could lead to conditions of stagflation has been argued particularly by Marxists (Sherman 1977, Kotz 1982).

In conclusion research points to considerable empirical and theoretical justification for substantially greater cyclical variation in profit margins in non-competitive economies. The evidence surveyed points to considerable price rigidity within the USA and UK, particularly in more oligopolistic sectors. This rigidity tends not to be a feature of either traditional Keynesian or neoclassical approaches to macroeconomics. Within a Kaleckian approach, this leads to a proposition of considerable cyclical instability in wage and profit shares. Static cross-section results such as those discussed earlier in this chapter may therefore be highly sensitive to the timing of the data used. The evidence presented and reviewed earlier for a negative relationship between wage share and industrial structure reinforces this implication. The purpose of Chapters 5, 6 and 7 is to examine in greater detail cyclical and secular variations in profitability and distributive shares.

NOTES

1. This is principally because disaggregated industry-level asset data are not collected by the annual Census of Production and are therefore rarely obtainable.
2. See Sawyer (1985b) Chap. 9 for a survey.
3. Waterson (1984) provides an up-to-date survey.
4. The results presented here were reported in an earlier and more extensive form in Henley (1987a).
5. The full sample of three-digit industries in the Census is 140 but our sample is reduced to 71 after removing industries with 'miscellaneous' in their titles, and after removing various industries for which no data on the advertising-sales ratio, union density or capital intensity were available.
6. This concentration ratio series has considerable advantages over other available series in that it makes precise adjustments (rather than 'guesstimates') for four common deficiencies in published concentration series. First it adjusts for the closeness of product groups within each industry, second for the geographical fragmentation of markets. The third adjustment is for where two products in separate industries are in close competition (for example, beet sugar and cane sugar) and finally an adjustment is made to reflect import penetration and export intensity.
7. In order to test the linear versus log-linear choice the Bera and McAleer test was computed (Maddala 1988). For the three-digit cross-section results (Table 3.1) the test was unable to reject either specification. For the four-digit results (Table 3.2) the log specification was preferred.
8. Additional estimations reported in Henley (1987a) but not reported here, where the capital intensity variable used is the fixed assets/value added ratio, give better determined estimates of the negative coefficient on concentration, although at the expense of poorer overall equation performance.
9. Blanchard and Fischer (1989, Chap. 8) provide a survey of these models.

4. The Influence of Collective Bargaining

TRADES UNIONS AND DISTRIBUTION: THE NEOCLASSICAL APPROACH

The issue of the influence of trades unions on the distribution of income between wages and profits is one that has been debated for a long time. Monopolistic influence in the labour market, in the form of trades union organization, can only be tackled within the neoclassical approach if product markets are perfectly competitive, to the extent that unions do not interfere with labour being paid its marginal product. Within the production function system it is possible to identify two possible ways through which trades unions might influence the profit-maximizing firm's choice of production technique.

The first possible influence is on factor input proportionality through a possible adjustment of relative factor prices. In a bargaining context, where unions negotiate a wage and then firms set employment levels in response to this wage, those firms can ensure that the chosen employment–wage combination was on their labour demand schedules and hence consistent with marginal productivity theory. For union impact on wage setting to influence distribution in favour of labour would require inelastic factor substitutability, particularly if technical progress is capital-using. So it can be seen that widespread econometric evidence of the 1960s and 1970s supporting a positive union–non-union earnings differential (Parsley 1980) is entirely consistent with the alleged stability of wage and profit shares over time. Union impact on relative income shares would be minimal in a world in which the elasticity of substitution between labour and capital was more or less equal to unity, or where any inelasticity in factor substitution was counterbalanced by a technological drift towards more capital-intensive production. Were union pressure on the wages paid by certain employers to result in lower profitability and higher wage share then perfect competition would ensure the eventual retreat of such firms from the market. Hence neoclassical economists have argued that trade union activity is irrelevant to the behaviour of distributional shares (Kerr 1957, Simler 1961). The only distributional shift that would result from trade union power would be between that part of labour share going to union workers and that going to non-union workers. This is exactly the point made in a celebrated paper by Levinson (1954), who observes stable income shares in the USA between 1929 and 1952 despite a fivefold growth in union membership.

The second possible influence of trades unions in the neoclassical framework is an indirect one, working through their potential impact on technical progress. Marginal productivity theory would break down if unions were able to raise wages and prevent substitution towards more capital-intensive production techniques, perhaps through preventing employment adjustment. In essence trades unions would be appropriating rent from a technological development. Again this would place unionized firms at a competitive disadvantage. Hence a precondition for such an effect on distribution to persist would either be the existence of employer monopoly power in the product market, or total union coverage of all firms in the relevant industry. However this proposition, given the econometric problems associated with time series production function estimation, seems very difficult to test rigorously.

BARGAINING POWER AND THE DEGREE OF MONOPOLY

Widening the field of view to allow for the existence of product market power considerably broadens the possibility for a potential union impact on distribution and profitability. This is because it allows for bargaining over monopolistic rent. Trade union activity might therefore be of consequence if it is able to affect the degree of monopoly.

Although Kalecki does not explicitly incorporate any formal model of the labour market into his degree of monopoly theory, it was noted in Chapter 2 that in a number of places he entertains the possibility that the power of organized labour may enter his framework as one of the structural conditions influencing the degree of monopoly. In early work (Kalecki 1938) he seems to be of the opinion that any trade union pressure on wage costs would simply be passed on by oligopolistic capitalist firms, through the mark-up, into higher prices. In a much later paper (published posthumously as Kalecki 1971b) he returns to the question of trade union influence on distribution. Clearly influenced by the growth in trade union power in many capitalist economies after the Second World War, he entertains the idea that the degree of monopoly may to some extent be kept down by the activity of trades unions:

A high ratio of profits to wages strengthens the bargaining position of trades unions in their demands for wage increases since higher wages are then compatible with 'reasonable profits' at existing price levels. If after such increases are granted prices should be raised, this will call forth new demands for wage increases... This adverse effect on the competitive position of a firm or an industry encourages the adoption of a policy of lower profit margins. Thus, the degree of monopoly will be kept down to some extent by the activity of trades unions, and this the more stronger the trades unions are. (Kalecki 1971a, p. 51)

However Kalecki certainly never developed a formal model of such trade union activity. He is characteristically terse about the precise way in which unions might affect the degree of monopoly:

High mark-ups in existence will encourage strong trade unions to bargain for higher wages as they know that firms can afford to pay them. If their demands are met but the functions f^1 are not changed, prices will also increase. This would lead to a new round of demand for higher wages and the process would go on with price levels constantly rising. But certainly an industry will not like such a process making its products more and more expensive and thus less competitive with the products of other industries... The power of trades unions manifests itself in the scale of wage rises demanded and achieved. If an increase in bargaining capacity is demonstrated by spectacular achievements, there is a downward shift in functions f and the mark-ups decline. A redistribution of national income from profits to wages will take place. (Kalecki 1971b, pp. 5-6)

It is unclear why one industry's product must compete with those of other industries, so this scenario is perhaps better expressed in the context of a single industry with a trade union bargaining with a group of firms within it. As far as an individual firm is concerned it might, particularly if the industry is an oligopolistic one, perceive that it faces a kinked demand curve – making it reluctant to raise unilaterally its product price for fear that rival firms will not match its price increases. Consequently if it faces an increase in the wages it must pay because of the presence at the bargaining table of a strong trade union, but its oligopolistic rivals are not at the same time faced with the same wage increase, then it will perhaps be reluctant to raise its own product price and so prefer to absorb the cost increase itself for fear of losing market share. In this case the trade union will make a distributional gain. As we shall discuss later this has implications for bargaining structure. A further aspect of this scenario is that the chances of a wage increase not being passed on into product price may be higher where the mark-up is already high. The degree of monopoly theory suggests this will be where concentration is high. So trade union impact on distribution may be dependent on the level of concentration.

Kalecki does attempt, albeit rather crudely by present standards, to present statistical evidence for the degree of monopoly theory. In Kalecki (1954) he examines long-run movements in wage share for the US manufacturing sector and for the UK in aggregate. For both the USA and UK up to the early 1930s, with the exception of the period of and just after the First World War, he argues that a rising degree of monopoly and a falling ratio of materials to wages costs tend over time to offset each other to leave wage share constant. After 1933 in the USA the degree of monopoly falls and Kalecki attributes this to the rising power of trades unions. Undoubtedly the 1930s saw considerable growth in union activity in the USA. However Levinson, already mentioned, doubts that unions affected distribution in aggregate, appealing instead to low interest rates and rents during the Roosevelt era. These squeezed rent and interest shares and allowed other income shares to rise.

Phelps-Brown and Hart (1952) entertained the possibility, though still at a time before widespread use of econometric estimation, that trades unions might have been responsible for the discrete shifts in the trend of manual workers' wage share in the UK observable this century. Although dated in statistical technique their paper warrants discussion. They envisage that any union impact on distribution is highly conditional on prevailing product market conditions. Implicitly therefore they point to a Kaleckian rather than a neoclassical explanation by suggesting that trades unions were able to affect income distribution where markets faced by producers were 'hard'. The adjective 'hard' is used in the sense that markets will not bear price increases warranted by a particular union-induced wage rise necessary to maintain profit margins. They first addressed themselves to the problem of identifying changes in distributional shifts in manual wage share from compositional changes brought about by the occupational shift in the work force towards salaried jobs. Once this is controlled for, Phelps-Brown and Hart find more evidence than at first appears for the secular stability of manual wage share. When purely distributional shifts occur they appear to occur at discrete points in time, rather than as slow changes in trend.

They go on to speculate about the effect of trades unions on manual wage share, under historically changing product market environments, and their contribution to these discrete shifts. They observe four such shifts, and infer the existence of two further shifts that must have occurred during each of the two World Wars during which reliable national income data were not collected. During two of the four observable shifts (1870 to 1872 and 1888 to 1889) wage share increases and there is an upward movement in the ratio of average earnings of wage-earners to national income per head. In the other two (1903 to 1905 and 1926 to 1928) wage share falls and the ratio of average earnings to national income per head also falls. All four points, Phelps-Brown and Hart argue, coincide with exceptional changes in trade union morale. The two falls in wage share coincide with the aftermaths of the Taff Vale Railway Case[2] and the 1926 General Strike and coalminers' lock-out. However Phelps-Brown and Hart question why no distributional shift resulted from the trade union membership collapse of 1879 to 1880 and during the exceptional periods of trade union growth between 1909 to 1913 and 1946 to 1950. They argue that these dates coincide with periods of 'soft' product markets and buoyant demand during which firms were able easily to diffuse union-won wage increases into higher final prices.

UNION–EMPLOYER BARGAINING: THEORETICAL CONSIDERATIONS

Recently interest in the impact of trades unions has experienced a considerable revival informed by recent theoretical work on union–employer bargaining.[3] In the context of potential product market monopolistic rent (an assumption not always clearly spelt out) profit–wage outcomes hinge on relative bargaining strength and on the bargaining agenda. The traditional case in which a 'monopoly' union picks its desired wage and the employer sets employment to equate this wage with marginal revenue product is a special case of a set of bargaining solutions bounded by the union's reservation wage (that in the non-unionized competitive sector) and the minimum level of profit that will avoid employer bankruptcy. A well known result is that any outcome on the labour demand curve is dominated in the Paretian sense by a locus of 'efficient' contracts off the labour demand curve. A contract on this locus can only be achieved if the bargaining agenda permits bargaining over both wages and the level of employment.

Following the usual convention we assume that the union seeks to maximize a concave utility function defined across the two arguments of wage and employment:

$$U = U(w, L)$$

where w is the wage (net of some fixed alternatively available income) and L is employment. The union faces a profit-maximizing firm. We assume for simplicity that the firm's capital stock is fixed. So profit is:

$$\Pi = \Pi(w, L) = R(L) - wL - \Pi' \qquad (4.1)$$

where $R(L)$ is the firm's revenue function, which is determined by the simple technical relationship between employment and output, and is assumed to be concave. Π' is the firm's reservation level of profit – that level of profit required to prevent exit from production. In the following analysis we will, without any loss of generality, assume Π' equals zero. In the 'labour demand curve' model bargaining is over the wage alone and the firm sets employment to maximize profits given the bargained wage. The bargaining problem can be expressed in conventional Nash terms as one of maximizing the weighted product of either side's objective function with respect to the decision variable, the weights being each side's relative bargaining strength:

$$\max_{w} \ \{\Pi(w, L)^{1-b}.U(w, L)^{b}\} \text{ subject to } w = R'(L) \quad (4.2)$$

where b is the relative bargaining strength parameter, $1 \geq b \geq 0$. b is the parameter governing the location of the bargain between the Nash threat points of each party, effectively determining the distribution of the monopolistic surplus. The function is maximized subject to the familiar marginal productivity constraint, which constrains any solution to the labour demand curve. As already mentioned, for any outcome on the labour demand there must exist a locus of Pareto-improving contracts which can be achieved if the bargaining agenda is widened to include employment. Now the bargaining problem becomes:

$$\max_{w, L} \ \{\Pi(w, L)^{1-b} . U(w, L)^{b}\} \quad (4.3)$$

where b now captures the new relative bargaining strengths under the new bargaining agenda. The general first-order conditions for the solution of both can be characterized as follows:

$$\Pi(w, L) = \frac{1-b}{b} \cdot \frac{-\dfrac{\delta\Pi(w,L)}{\delta w}}{\dfrac{\delta U(w,L)}{\delta w}} U(w, L) \quad (4.4a)$$

$$\Pi(w, L) = \frac{1-b}{b} \cdot \frac{-\dfrac{\delta\Pi(w,L)}{\delta L}}{\dfrac{\delta U(w,L)}{\delta L}} U(w, L) \quad (4.4b)$$

In the wage-only bargaining case the bargaining parties are, of course, additionally constrained by the marginal productivity condition. For the wage–employment bargaining case it is a well established result that the slope of the contract curve is non-negative (Oswald 1985). Therefore union utility must be increasing in both wage and employment so $\delta U(w, L)/\delta w$ and $\delta U(w, L)/\delta L$ are both non-negative. Therefore the relationship between the relative bargaining strength parameter and profits, i.e. whether an increase in union power reduces profits, hinges on the sign of the two incremental profit functions. Specifically for $\Pi(w, L)$ and b to be negatively related, the incremental profit functions must be negative. Referring back to equation 4.1 the incremental profit functions for changes in wage and employment for the wage–employment bargaining case are hence:

$$\frac{\delta\Pi(w, L)}{\delta w} = -L \qquad\qquad (4.5a)$$

and

$$\frac{\delta\Pi(w, L)}{\delta L} = R'(L) - w \qquad\qquad (4.5b)$$

Since for any 'off-the-demand' curve solution it must be the case that $w > R'(L)$ (i.e. wage is above marginal revenue product) then both incremental functions are non-positive and a negative relationship will exist between profit and the bargaining strength parameter b.

The wage-only bargaining case is more complicated since wage and employment are now no longer independent of each other, being linked through the marginal productivity condition, $w = R'(L)$. If we substitute this condition into the expression for firm profit the incremental profit function with respect to employment becomes:

$$\frac{\delta\Pi(w, L)}{\delta L} = -L.R''(L) \qquad\qquad (4.6)$$

which, since $R(L)$ is assumed concave, is positive. However we can no longer say that the incremental utility functions are non-negative since the solution is constrained by the marginal productivity condition. Therefore if employment increases within the relevant employment range then union utility must fall and so the incremental union utility function with respect to changes in employment must be negative. Hence the negative relationship between bargaining strength and profits still holds. Strictly speaking the increase in union bargaining strength will at best (from the employer's point of view) have no effect on profits. This would occur where the union had already succeeded in negotiating a wage that maximized its utility i.e. at a point of tangency between the labour demand and the union's indifference curve map (point A in Figure 4.1). This case is usually referred to as the 'monopoly union' case (Oswald 1985). Even if bargaining strength were to increase for some reason then the union would have no incentive to negotiate a wage above w_{max}. So we can say that in the

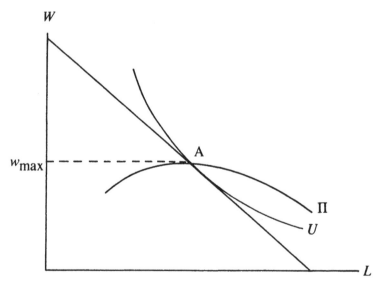

Figure 4.1 The maximum wage under wage-only union–firm bargaining

wage–employment bargaining case if union bargaining strength increases profits must fall, but in the wage-only bargaining case profits may fall or remain constant.

This conclusion no longer holds if we consider the case where the firm's product price is determined by a fixed mark-up on unit labour cost. This is of course an extreme case, implying, if the profit-maximization assumption is to be preserved, an iso-elastic product demand schedule. We consider it because it is useful for illustrative purposes, encapsulating the case described by Kalecki where the firm simply keeps passing on wage increases into higher product prices. In reality conditions might well lie between the two extremes of fixed product price as above and fixed mark-up. The extent to which conditions would lie between the two would depend on the nature and extent of the firm's product market power. We can in the fixed mark-up case specify the firm's revenue function as follows:

$$R(L) = qku \tag{4.7}$$

where q is output, k the fixed mark-up and u unit variable cost. If we maintain the simple case where variable costs comprise solely wage costs then $u = wL/q$. Therefore the firm's profit function can be written as:

$$\Pi = (k - 1)wL \tag{4.8}$$

For the case of wage and employment bargaining the incremental profit functions are now:

$$\frac{\delta\Pi(w, L)}{\delta w} = (k - 1)L \tag{4.9a}$$

and

$$\frac{\delta\Pi(w, L)}{\delta L} = (k - 1)w \tag{4.9b}$$

Since k must be greater than unity both expressions are positive and so referring back to equations 4.4a and 4.4b the relationship between profits and union bargaining strength must be a positive one. The intuition behind this is that as the union is able to raise the wage bill through increased bargaining strength the firm's revenue rises in absolute terms by more than the increase in the wage bill because it is determined by applying the fixed mark-up to the wage bill. The firm's profit–revenue ratio (equivalent in this case to profit share) will remain constant. Intuitively then the union will only be able to bring about a reduction in the firm's profit–revenue ratio if the effect of its increased bargaining power on wages is able at the same time to place sufficient downward pressure on the mark-up.

In the 'labour demand curve' case, where bargaining is over the wage alone, the firm's profit function becomes:

$$\Pi = (k - 1)R'(L)\,L \tag{4.10}$$

Differentiation gives the following incremental profit function for changes in employment:

$$\frac{\delta\Pi(w, L)}{\delta L} = (k - 1)(R'(L) + LR''(L))$$

which rearranges as:

$$\frac{\delta\Pi(w, L)}{\delta L} = (k - 1)\frac{1}{w}\left[1 + \frac{1}{e_w}\right] \tag{4.11}$$

where e_w is the wage elasticity of demand for labour. From this we can see that the incremental profit function is only negative if $e_w < -1$. If again we assume that the union will not negotiate a wage that gives a wage employment solution with a level of utility that can be raised if employment is increased then we see from equation 4.4b that profits and union bargaining strength are only inversely related in the unlikely case that labour demand is elastic. So once more increases in union bargaining strength can, if labour demand is inelastic, only result in lower firm profit if the union's bargaining pressure is able to reduce the size of the mark-up. Again if the union has already obtained a wage level corresponding to the point of tangency between its utility function and the labour demand curve then increases in bargaining strength will produce no change in the wage–employment outcome and hence no change in profits.

Implicit in this rather simplified assessment of union impact on profitability is an assumption that trades unions are primarily concerned with maximizing the money wages of their members, or with optimizing their perceived trade-off between wages and employment. We should subject this to the scrutiny of the considerable literature on trade union objectives. One long-standing objection to a purely economistic conception of trades unions as unitary maximizing agents is that of Ross (1948). Arthur Ross's view was that the heterogeneous nature of the membership of trades unions means that different groups within the union will have different objectives (e.g. older workers being more concerned about early retirement provision than wage levels). The consequence of this is that union policies tend to be formulated in a political decision-making process and so to argue in favour of trades unions possessing, for example, a simple wage bill maximand ignores the complex political pressures and attitudes that feed into union policy making. John Dunlop's response (1950), which sparked off the famous Dunlop–Ross debate, was to argue that union leaders are capable of formulating and pursuing economic objectives.

Recent theoretical work on the economic modelling of union activity has generated a revival in this debate (for example Turnbull 1988a, 1988b, Disney and Gospel 1989). In particular the 'new' microeconomic theory of unionism has raised the issue of the empirical validity of employment bargaining. As Oswald (1984), Oswald and Turnbull (1985) show, explicit agreements on employment levels in the UK and the USA are rare. Union pressure on employment levels is more likely to occur through implicit working arrangements on manning levels, etc. Known lay-off procedures, operating perhaps through seniority rules, may render the 'median voter' union member unconcerned about employment levels. In such models the union's preferences would be characterized by those of the median voter and so generate efficient contracts that are coincident with the labour demand curve. Bargaining over employment levels under these circumstances cannot therefore improve the union's position.

At a more general level Manning (1987) argues that the failure of unions and firms to reach 'efficient bargains' under which employment will be higher than in the 'labour demand' case is due to 'differential control'. Unions within the capitalist economy have considerable power in the sphere of wage setting but little in the sphere of employment determination. He cites a number of reasons for this. First union organization, particularly in the UK, is often geared towards bargaining at the multi-employer level, a level at which trades unions are unlikely to be able to exert much influence over establishment-level employment. A second reason concerns the credibility of union action over employment issues. Known seniority provisions mean that marginal employment adjustments will present little risk of lay-off to the majority of union members and so strike action in opposition to such adjustments will be difficult to implement. Furthermore information about employment issues may be asymmetrically distributed between unions and employers. Consequently unions may find it difficult to verify the true employment consequences of wage-bargaining policies, and may be content to leave employment issues to managerial control.

The preceding analysis has suggested that the relationship between union power and employer profitability will be conditioned by the type of bargaining model in operation, and product market structural conditions. In oligopolistic industrial sectors it is reasonable to suppose that firms enjoy considerable control over their product-pricing decisions and so we may suppose that pricing to some extent follows the mark-up case. Hence it is plausible that the union–firm bargaining process is unrelated to the division of monopolistic quasi-rents. This would imply that the nature of union–firm bargaining would have no effect on the economic performance of the industry, except perhaps to exacerbate inflationary pressure on final product prices. However, as already stated, in practice mark-up conventions may be circumscribed by market conditions, allowing firms to divert some but not all of the effect of increased union bargaining strength on to their consumers. We must therefore appeal to empirical work to shed light on any relationship between union strength and profitability and income shares.

UNION POWER AND PROFITS: EMPIRICAL EVIDENCE

There has in recent years begun to emerge a stream of empirical work, almost exclusively for the USA, addressing the question of the impact of unions on profits. Addison and Hirsch (1989) in their survey of this literature collate the results of sixteen such studies using American data. Of these sixteen five use published industry level cross-section data, and the remainder firm or establishment-level survey data. Despite wide variation in model specification and wide variation in the profit measure employed there would appear to be a very strong conformity of results, namely supporting the conclusion that union presence significantly lowers profit rates and price–cost margins. As reported by Addison and Hirsch, of the industry-level studies Freeman (1983) estimates a reduction in price–cost margins of between 13 and 19 per cent as a result of a switch from 0 to 100 per cent union coverage. The other studies by Voos and Michel (1986), Domowitz *et al.* (1986b, 1988) and Karier (1985) obtain corresponding estimates of between 22 and 25 per cent.

We can highlight a number of important themes to emerge from these studies. The first is that the conventional effect of concentration on profitability is considerably understated in regression equations that fail to control for trade union strength. This is because much of the monopolistic rent obtained from market dominance is appropriated by trade union activity. Karier (1985), on the basis of cross-section evidence for 1972, suggests that the scale of the underestimation of the effect of concentration on profits may be as high as 65 per cent. Consistent with this he estimates that the proportion of potential monopoly profits actually retained by concentrated industries is as low as 32 per cent; unions appropriate the remaining 68 per cent. A more recent study by the same author (Karier 1988), using US industry-level cross-section data for 1972, additionally controls for the effect of import penetration on potential profits, and concludes that unions appropriate 47 per cent of those potential profits. Salinger (1984), from a sample of 175 American firms in 1979, estimates this proportion to be as high as 77 per cent in a typical firm. The point that the union impact on monopoly profits is highest in more concentrated industries is made by most of these studies. Domowitz *et al.* (1986) is the principal exception. Because unions are more likely to organize in firms or industries where the potential for appropriation of monopoly profit is greater these estimates of the union impact may exhibit downward simultaneity bias. Indeed Addison and Hirsch report that where researchers compare estimated results with those obtained using simultaneous estimation procedures the union impact becomes even larger in the latter case.

To date the only comparable study for the UK is that of Machin (1988b). Machin uses data on a sample of 145 British firms pooled over the two years 1984 and 1985. Union presence is measured by a dummy variable indicating whether or not each firm recognizes trades unions for collective bargaining purposes. The profit measure is a trading profit–sales ratio. Union recognition has the effect of reducing measured profitability by 28 per cent. This would suggest that union impact on profitability in Britain is rather smaller than that generally observed in the USA. Machin's results also strongly support the suggestion that union impact on profits is highest where firms enjoy greater market dominance.

Interestingly the sole study to find a significant positive union impact on profitability is for a pooled sample of 62 metalworking firms in the Federal Republic of Germany in 1977 and 1979 by Fitzroy and Kraft (1985). They model hourly wages, managerial salaries, union density and the rate of return on capital within a simultaneous equation framework, and obtain a statistically significant positive coefficient on union density in the profitability equation. Their model controls for a number of qualitative features of the companies, such as labour turnover, extent of managerial hierarchy and existence of works councils. The existence of a works council significantly reduces profitability. These results suggest that participation mechanisms may replace the role of trades unions in allowing for redistribution of monopoly rent, and that as a result unionization is a considerably less effective vehicle of worker bargaining power in West Germany. Fitzroy and Kraft argue that unionization may occur as a presumably ineffective defensive move by workers facing an efficient management making high profits.

UNION POWER AND LABOUR SHARE:
EMPIRICAL EVIDENCE

Traditionally the conclusion that trades unions both in the UK and the USA serve to raise wages above competitive levels was thought to be well established.[4] The most recent and sophisticated studies which control for differences in the characteristics of unionized and non-unionized workers (Stewart 1983, Shah 1984 for the UK) suggest that the true differential may be quite small and in many industries, such as coal and petroleum products manufacture and leather goods (Stewart *op. cit.*), may be non-existent. Observed raw differentials are likely to be the result of compensating differentials for the higher average skill levels of unionized workers. It is however rather difficult to draw any inferences from these studies on the effect of union power on wage share.

The analysis has shown that the presence of a union 'wage gap' is not in itself sufficient to guarantee a union impact on distribution. Any impact will be dependent on the nature of price formation. The overall impact on distribution will also be conditioned by technological conditions, and particularly the effect of union presence on productivity. However it seems likely that this effect may be of rather marginal quantitative significance. The direction and extent of the effect has been the subject of considerable debate since the 'Harvard School' proposition of a beneficial union productivity effect put forward by, among others, Richard Freeman and James Medoff (Freeman 1976, Freeman and Medoff 1984). As tests have become more refined it seems likely that this proposition cannot be empirically sustained for the USA.[5] The only formal econometric test of the relationship between union activity and productivity for the UK (Machin 1988a) finds that union impact is largely neutral. For those convinced by the beneficial 'voice' role of trades unions proposed by Freeman and Medoff this result for the UK is still not surprising given the rather more antagonistic attitudes held by British trades unions and employers than their American counterparts. Fitzroy and Kraft (1985) on the basis of their empirical work for West Germany point out that the relationship between unionization and efficiency is wrapped up with the efficiency effects of formalized labour-management institutions. In an industrial system such as that in

West Germany well established worker participation procedures may well explain an observed positive relationship between union representation and plant-level efficiency.

Early cross-section tests of the Kaleckian distribution model, reviewed in Chapter 3, did not tend to control for variations in union strength. Cowling and Molho (1982) included various proxies for union power in their wage share estimations for the UK. Unionism was variously measured as strike intensity, strike duration, union membership and collective agreement coverage. As discussed in Chapter 3 their results show that concentration has a clear inverse relationship with wage share. Although trade union activity may be able to raise wage share above what it would have been in its absence it is certainly not able to offset fully the impact of product market monopoly power. Their coefficient estimates for 1968 suggest that a 10 per cent increase in union membership is likely to lead to a 1.5 per cent increase in wage share. They also observed a significant positive effect on salary share (i.e. the income share of non-production staff) of an increase in union membership.

Conyon (1988) uses a variable measuring collective agreement coverage as a proxy for union strength in his pooled cross-section estimations for UK manufacturing industry in the 1980s. Collective agreement coverage is arguably a better proxy for union strength than a measure of union density or strike intensity. Such measures may ignore the possibility of important spillover effects to non-union workers who nevertheless receive the union-negotiated wage. Increased strike intensity may be seen as indicative of failure on the part of trades unionists to obtain their demands. Also Conyon makes the important point that a collective agreement coverage measure is more likely to be exogenous to the wage-setting process than a union activity measure. His results for the period 1980 to 1984 display a very well determined positive impact of collective agreement coverage on production worker wage share. His results also show a quantitatively larger effect than those of Cowling and Molho. In the roughly comparable single-year cross-section estimating equations he obtains an elasticity of wage share with respect to union membership of around 0.3.

The labour share regressions reported in Chapter 3 for the more aggregated three-digit cross-section sample of 71 US manufacturing industries in 1972 conditioned for collective agreement coverage using the data of Freeman and Medoff (1979). For the narrowest measure of labour share, namely production worker wage share, the union effect is well determined and suggests a positive effect of remarkably similar size to that obtained for the UK by Cowling and Molho. A 10 per cent increase in collective agreement coverage leads to a 1.7 per cent increase in production worker wage share of value added. The effect is rather smaller in magnitude for the broader measures of wage share, and for the wage and salary share measure (WS2) only statistically significant at the 10 per cent level.

Time series estimation of the wage share, concentration and unionism relationship suggests that the aggregate positive effect of unionism observed from cross-section studies holds up well for particular industries. Kalleberg *et al.* (1984) conclude for the American printing industry between 1946 and 1978 that the proportion of workers unionized does appear to affect positively production worker wage share of value added. Henley (1986b) reports results for the American automobile industry for the period 1949 to 1980 and obtains a positive elasticity of production worker wage share with respect to union density of between 0.3 and 0.4. Sub-sample results suggest that union impact on wage share was strongest in the American automobile industry in the 1950s and early 1960s.

The form of bargaining structure within which trades unions press for wage gains may be of importance. The discussion of Kalecki's own ideas, earlier in this chapter, points to the importance of asymmetries between firms in the nature of collective agreements reached. Principally we may be able to draw a distinction between a structure in which the trade union negotiates with all firms simultaneously and a structure where a separate bargain is struck with each firm. In the latter case, assuming that spillover effects of one bargain to another are minimal, it may be difficult for the firm to pass on cost increases into final prices and so the trade union may be able to make a distributional gain.

The British experience of the 1960s, as identified by the Donovan Commission (1968), was that of the growth of the two-tier collective bargaining system.[6] The two-tier system involved a national industry-wide basic pay agreement on top of which local trades union branches would negotiate establishment or enterprise-specific premia. If we take a given wage increase and assess its effect on income distribution we might expect a greater impact (or at least some impact) on the degree of monopoly where that wage increase has at least in part been achieved through a firm- or plant-specific agreement, and any productivity deal does not outweigh this price effect on distribution. However the question of relative union power under different bargaining arrangements is important since the trade union may find it easier to negotiate a given wage increase under one arrangement rather than another. If plant-specific bargaining is associated with an increase in union power at the bargaining table then it may well have resulted in a distributional improvement. So the two-tier bargaining arrangements prevalent in the UK in the late 1960s and early 1970s may provide an example of conditions under which labour power was able to influence the degree of monopoly. Early rather crude work on the British union wage differential in the 1970s by Mulvey (1976) suggested that collective bargaining was only able to raise wage levels where bargaining contained some plant-specific element, either as a plant-only agreement or as a plant-specific premium negotiated above a national deal. Henley (1986b) reports, using UK cross-section data for the 1970s, results that suggest that the impact of collective bargaining on wage share may have been limited to where two-tier bargaining was in operation.

We must however consider the possibility that bargaining structure is endogenous to the determination of wage share. Both firms and unions will have a preferred bargaining structure[7] and the observed outcome will depend on the relative strength of the two sides. If union wage demands result in a fall in the degree of monopoly mark-up then firms may well respond by attempting to switch to a bargaining structure more favourable to their interests. Hence the development of single-employer multi-plant agreements in the late 1970s as identified by Brown (1981) might be seen as a counter-response to a possible distributional gain achieved as a result of two-tier bargaining. Alternatively the switch in bargaining structure in the late 1970s in the UK might be seen as a 'political' move by union leaders to reassert central union control over powerful shop floor negotiating units.

ASSESSMENT AND IMPLICATIONS FOR MACROECONOMIC PERFORMANCE

The evidence on the impact of union activity on industrial profitability would seem to come down very strongly in favour of a significant depressant effect being generated by trades union activity. This is particularly so for the USA. The evidence on union impact on wage share supports this. However the strength of this result is problematic. First it seems inconsistent with the generally rather small average union impact on wages. But of course a small positive union impact on wages is likely to generate a proportionately much larger effect on profits. The most sophisticated studies, using individual worker-level micro data and analysing the effect on individual union status, find that the union–non-union wage differential is by any standards rather small. On top of this there would seem now to exist a reasonable consensus that any union impact on productivity both in the UK and the USA is largely neutral. How do we therefore explain the union–profit relationship? The most plausible explanation is that it is capturing what Lewis (1983) describes as an 'extent of unionism' effect. This means that the union effect is measuring the influence of a whole range of important differences between unionized and non-unionized industries or companies, such as differences in work force characteristics, in managerial control, and in technology. There is therefore a need for studies to examine profit per worker at the micro level, in order to assess the extent to which the individual worker benefits from the redistribution of monopolistic rent if his own status changes from non-union to union. Following on from this we as yet have little or no idea if the average redistributive effect of trades unions conceals a range of a few 'haves' and many 'have-nots', as appears to be the case with the union wage effect.

What of the macroeconomic implications? As shown in Chapter 3 macroeconomic modellers within the orthodox neo-Keynesian tradition are increasingly incorporating some degree of product market imperfection into their work. A small number of authors have recently attempted to incorporate the role of union–firm bargaining into macroeconomic models. In Britain probably the most well known of these is the Layard–Nickell model of the UK aggregate labour market (Layard and Nickell 1985, 1986a). At the heart of this model is a framework of real wage and unemployment determination governed by the interaction of real product wage aspirations of trades unions (the 'target' real wage) and the feasible mark-up of nominal prices on nominal wages attainable by price-setting firms. Equilibrium occurs at a level of output (unemployment) where unemployment is sufficiently high to equate trades unions' real wage aspirations with firms' ability to pay. Implicitly therefore unemployment regulates conditions on the supply side of the economy in order to bring about an 'acceptable' distribution of income between wages and profits. This equilibrium level of unemployment is referred to as the non-accelerating inflation rate of unemployment or NAIRU for short (see Figure 4.2). In their empirical testing of the model Layard and Nickell find some role for trade union power (measured by a crude time series of the union–non-union wage differential) in explaining the rise in unemployment in the UK in the 1970s and early 1980s. However they do not control empirically for firms' price-setting behaviour and so make no assessment of the effect

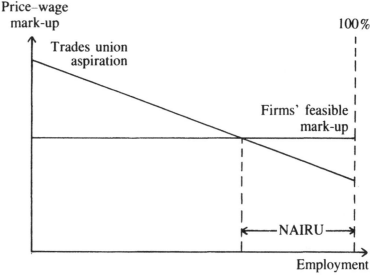

Figure 4.2   Determination of unemployment in the Layard–Nickell model

of product market power on aggregate output and unemployment. The relationship between wages and prices (the real product wage) is in the Layard–Nickell model exclusively determined by the supply side of the economy. Aggregate demand (or aggregate capacity utilization) is exogenously determined by such factors as government fiscal stance, world trade volume and international price competitiveness, although eventually has to adjust to the NAIRU.

From a Kaleckian point of view the absence of any relationship between the structural conditions determining wages and prices and aggregate demand through the role of capacity utilization and investment is a serious omission. In the Layard–Nickell model an increase in trade union power would necessitate a higher level of unemployment to discipline wage demands so as to maintain equilibrium between the target real wage and firms' feasible mark-up. However an increase in real wages resulting from higher trade union aspirations will influence aggregate demand. One effect on aggregate demand will come about through the effect on total savings of a redistribution from profit to wage income. A second effect will come about through the effect of reduced profitability on the attractiveness of investment. Whether one effect dominates the other may depend on the level of capacity utilization prevailing in the economy. The overall effect may be to exacerbate or to mitigate the stagnationary effect of the increase in union bargaining power. Models which incorporate these effects formally are presented by Rowthorn (1977), Sawyer (1982a, 1982b) and Taylor (1985).

In the dynamic context variations in trade union bargaining power may paradoxically contribute to cyclical movements in the capitalist economy. In the early part of a cyclical expansion, as unemployment falls trade union power rises and the redistributive consequences of this change will stimulate further growth in output and a further reduction in unemployment. However as the evidence of Chapters 6 and 7 will demonstrate, profitability tends typically to peak prematurely in each business cycle. This premature peak may stifle the attractiveness of further investment and eventually lead to the downturn in output. Taylor (1983, 1985) formally shows the conditions under which such cyclical behaviour would be generated. So, although the cross-section microeconomic evidence reviewed in this chapter suggests that monopolistic rent-seeking activities of capitalist enterprises may be quite substantially mitigated by the bargaining power of trades unions, conflict over income distribution may contribute to potentially poor macroeconomic performance and instability. Such a conclusion contrasts sharply with the orthodox neoclassical view of the irrelevance of collective bargaining.

NOTES

1. These are the functions determining the relationship between costs and prices, in other words the degree of monopoly.
2. The Taff Vale Case established that trades unions could be held responsible for damages to their employers as a result of strike action.
3. Oswald (1985) provides a comprehensive survey of recent developments in the microeconomic theory of the trade union.
4. Comprehensive surveys of the union wage differential literature are provided by Parsley (1980), Lewis (1983) and Hirsch and Addison (1986).
5. Surveys of the American evidence on the relationship between unionization and productivity are provided by Addison (1983) and Addison and Hirsch (1989).
6. Although the growth of two-tier bargaining structures is linked with productivity bargaining, by the 1970s the productivity bargain had largely become a means by which incomes policies could be circumvented (McKersie and Hunter 1973). Some debate exists in the industrial relations literature as to whether two-tier bargaining represented a shift in power towards or away from trades unions. Cliff argues that productivity bargains were 'part of a major offensive by the employing class to shift the balance of forces permanently in their direction' (Cliff 1970, p. 3). Terry (1977) and Gallie (1978) both argue that productivity bargaining represented a potential gain in power for labour since it shifted influence towards shop floor representatives, strengthening rank and file control over management decisions and away from management by placing bargaining responsibility further down the managerial hierarchy.
7. For example, Marginson (1985) explores this question of the determination of bargaining structure in the context of the development of the multi-divisional firm.

5. Income Shares and Profitability Crisis in the PostWar Period: Methodology

Chapter 3 examined a number of microeconomic aspects of the behaviour of firms under oligopolistic conditions. The empirical work surveyed suggested that under such conditions pricing was largely insensitive to demand conditions, and that oligopolists tend to absorb the cyclical movements in cost conditions through profit margins. In this chapter and the two subsequent chapters we look more closely at the cyclical behaviour of profitability, and the way in which distribution and aggregate demand conditions contribute to secular movements in profitability in the postwar US and UK economies. This exercise is important because the rate of profit is seen by many economists as a critical indicator of macroeconomic performance influencing future profit expectations and in turn the prospects for future investment and economic growth.

It is clear that both the British and American economies experienced a sustained profits 'squeeze' throughout the 1960s and into the 1970s. In the context of the UK over the last fifteen years a good deal of paper and ink has been expended in attempting to establish the empirical validity and causes of the asserted profits squeeze.[1] In contrast it now seems that the British corporate sector is currently enjoying something of a profits revival. Similarly the question of the profits squeeze in the late 1960s and 1970s in the USA has also been much discussed, particularly by the Brookings Institution[2] and by the Union of Radical Political Economists.[3] Although much discussed in a very diverse literature there appears to be little consensus on an explanation. Broadly speaking we might divide candidate explanations into two, not mutually exclusive, groups. For expositional purposes we will

81

term them 'demand-side' theories and 'supply-side' theories, and in crude terms we might see this distinction corresponding to movements in the 'realization curve' and 'profits curve' respectively developed in Chapter 2. A second important distinction is that between cyclical explanations for movements in income shares and profitability and explanations for secular movements.

On the demand side explanations focus on the effect of falling aggregate demand on levels of capacity utilization so lowering the rate of output to capital and therefore initiating a decline in the rate of realizable profit on capital employed. Supply-side explanations focus on secular shifts in and shocks to the cost structure of producers which cannot be passed on into higher prices. These might be crudely captured through a squeeze on the share of profits in output. Within supply-side explanations we might also include those explanations which focus on the effect on accelerating inflation on the price–costs relationship of producers. In many respects these two broad explanations should not be seen as independent of each other and so we should wary of forcing the distinction too far.

Clearly secular changes in product demand should not place pressure on long-term profitability if firms in the medium term can make adjustments to fixed production inputs in response to necessary demand-induced changes in their output levels. Short-term cyclical changes in output will be reflected in capacity utilization as output levels rise and fall but fixed costs remain constant. For falling capacity utilization to provide an explanation of secular changes in profitability would require some form of asymmetric adjustment of inputs to output levels in each expansion and contraction, perhaps from some resulting long-term hoarding of productive potential above levels required to meet immediate demand. Bowers, Deaton and Turk (1982) provide evidence on labour hoarding. Explanations for such behaviour might, for example, depend on implicit contracting with labour input suppliers, adjustment costs associated with contract renegotiation, redundancy provision, etc., and persistent expectation errors about future demand conditions. Bowers, Deaton and Turk themselves point to production and organizational inflexibilities which lead firms to 'excess hiring' in a recession. However it seems unlikely that such explanations are sustainable as explanations of long-term movements in profitability. The stagnation theory of Steindl (1952), discussed in Chapter 2, identifies a process of product market monopolization as being responsible for a spiral of declining capacity utilization and investment. The effect of falling capacity utilization on investment is also a feature of the work of stagnationist Keynesians such as Domar (1946). So although the initial source of decline in capacity utilization may be attributable to a demand-side shock, the process is sustained through the supply-side responses of capitalists. Alternatively, as discussed in Chapter 3, recent developments in the theory of entry deterrence point to the use of excess capacity as a strategic credible signal of a willingness to expand output in the face of entry. In contrast to this explanation of a positive link between profitability and capacity utilization Cowling (1983) suggests that as capacity utilization falls oligopolistic firms may respond by raising levels of implicit collusion in order to try to preserve profit margins. Thus any relationship between falling capacity utilization and profitability decline is likely to be a transient phenomenon, as in the longer term firms respond by establishing closer levels of implicit collusion. The relationship between government spending and profitability, through the effect of the former on aggregate demand, may also be an important factor (Baran and Sweezy 1966).

It is also in principle possible to posit a public sector 'crowding-out' hypothesis for falling profitability. This is potentially one implication of the contentious debate initiated by Bacon and Eltis (1978). This can be seen as providing a demand-side explanation of falling profitability, through its focus on the 'crowding-out' of private investment and production. This might result through rising competition between governmental and private sectors for available labour resources, or through competition for investment funds in capital markets. It may also place pressure on profitability and less directly through the effect of higher tax burdens, made necessary as a result of rising public expenditure, which will lower corporate profits directly, and indirectly may place upward pressure on real wages due to rising personal and indirect tax burdens. The corresponding argument to this might be that profitability revival may be explained by a reduction in the tendency for government to crowd out. One manifestation of this may be found in recent policy directed, particularly in Britain, towards privatization in its broadest sense. As central and local government withdraw from responsibility for large areas of provision of goods and services, and initiates moves towards 'contracting out' of those for which it retains responsibility, the effect may be to increase and improve the opportunities for profit generation by the private capitalist sector. This argument stands in sharp contrast to Baran and Sweezy's underconsumptionist ideas which argue that rising government expenditure may provide capitalists with a useful 'external market' in which to realize profit. However Kalecki (1943) in his discussion of the political–business cycle points out a possible ambivalence on the part of capitalists to rising government expenditure, which is highlighted by this distinction between the crowding-out effect and the external market effect (see Chapter 8).

Finally a number of commentators have identified the rising tide of international competition during the 1960s and 1970s as placing pressure on domestic firms' profit margins (see especially Glyn and Sutcliffe 1972). However a number of objections to this idea have been raised, some relating to Glyn and Sutcliffe's empirical formulation of this hypothesis (see Cowling 1982). The most important is that the structure of foreign competition is crucial to this argument. A couple of rather dated cross-sectional studies for the UK fail to find a significant negative relationship between domestic profitability and import penetration (Khalilzadeh-Shirazi, 1974, Hart and Morgan, 1977). On the other hand Hitiris (1978) argues that such studies misspecify the relationship between profitability and import penetration, demonstrating that of importance is the effective rate of protection enjoyed by domestic producers. He finds that such a measure exerts a significant influence on profit margins in UK manufacturing industry. Studies for the USA have also found a significant relationship between profitability and foreign competition (Caves 1985). As international capital has developed an increasingly transnational base it is no longer clear that imports can be seen as a competitive discipline (Sugden 1983). Cowling and Sugden (1987) argue that a significant proportion of imports into Britain tend to be under the control of domestic multinationals. The extent to which this has attenuated the competitive discipline of foreign trade is the subject of debate (Auerbach and Skott 1988).

As far as our search for an explanation for secular, as opposed to cyclical, movements in profitability is concerned, 'supply-side' explanations are likely to prove more fruitful, although as we have discussed above it is conceptually possible for a demand shock to initiate a secular movement in profitability, although that secular trend is likely to be perpetuated by 'supply-side' reactions from capitalists.

Commentators on the 1960s profits squeeze have focused on an array on differing changes in industrial cost structures. One of the earliest, and most commonly discussed since, is the rising bargaining power of labour hypothesis. The seminal exposition of this idea is provided by Glyn and Sutcliffe (1972), whose argument in simple terms was that British capitalism was caught between the anvil of increasingly powerful organized trades unions and the hammer of international competition. The rising labour bargaining strength argument is, they argue, manifest in the rising share of labour income in GDP in the UK in the 1950s and 1960s. Fixed exchange rates allowed this to happen by preventing domestic producers from raising prices and maintaining competitiveness through currency devaluation. In essence this theory associates the profits squeeze with a failure of productivity increases to keep pace with real wage rises. Glyn and Sutcliffe highlight three changes in the nature of collective bargaining over the period in question. The first was the shift away from national industry-wide wage bargaining, towards increasing use of company or plant-specific supplemental bargaining which they argue has generated an earnings drift. The second change was the growing strength of shop stewards, with its associated transfer of power away from management, and the third was the increasing frequency and duration of strikes.

THE CYCLICAL BEHAVIOUR OF PROFITS: A REVIEW

Comprehensive work on the analysis of the cyclical behaviour of the economy in the USA goes back to the pioneering work of Wesley Mitchell at the National Bureau of Economic Research in the 1940s and 1950s (Burns and Mitchell 1946, Mitchell 1951). Recent work and debate on cyclical movements in profitability follows a similar, though somewhat simplified, methodology. Mitchell's work was concerned with an elaborate analysis of different stages of business cycles and the movement of key economic variables over those cycle stages. Boddy and Crotty (1975), Hahnel and Sherman (1982a, 1982b) and Sherman (1986, 1987) preserve the Mitchell nine-stage cycle breakdown. Other work, in particular Weisskopf (1979) and subsequent responses, adopt a simpler three-stage cycle breakdown and it is this simpler approach that we shall follow in the two subsequent chapters.

Hahnel and Sherman (1982b) identify three conflicting hypotheses concerning the movement of income shares over the business cycle. The 'wage-lag' hypothesis suggests that as the economy enters an expansion phase productivity improves rapidly and real wages fail to keep pace therefore allowing profit share to rise. A number of factors may contribute to this pattern. First, technological improvements, it is argued, tend to arise during upswings rather than downswings. Second, workers may feel little reason to resist productivity improvements during the upswing if real wages are rising, albeit at a slower rate. In the downswing real wage cuts are more likely to be opposed, and public opinion is more likely to be sympathetic to such opposition.

In contrast the 'reserve army' hypothesis would in its crudest form predict a countercyclical movement in profit share. As unemployment falls during the upswing worker militancy increases and squeezes profit share. Boddy and Crotty (1975) outline a more sophisticated cyclical version of this reserve army or wage-push explanation for the profits squeeze in the American context. They identify the premature peak in profitability, before the peak in the level of real output, in postwar American business cycles. They attribute this premature peak to the cyclical behaviour of unit labour costs. This, they argue, can be attributed to the cyclical mopping up of the reserve army, leading to an 'increasingly obstreperous' labour force as the economy approaches the peak of each cycle.

The third hypothesis is the 'overhead-labour' hypothesis which attributes the procyclical movement in profit share to procyclical movements in overall labour productivity.[4] This in turn is brought about by the under-utilization of overhead labour during the recession. As output falls capitalists fire production staff but, at least initially, hold on to overhead labour in anticipation of a future upturn in business activity. Productivity therefore falls and with it the share of profits. In the upswing a reverse process occurs.

Important seminal work by Thomas Weisskopf (1979), much discussed and debated by subsequent writers, has attempted to account for the behaviour of the aggregate rate of profit in the postwar American economy and encapsulates each of these hypotheses. The Weisskopf methodology adopts a simple decomposition of the rate of profit on capital into basic constituent components and shows how the behaviour of the profit rate is composed from the behaviour of the components. Hence Weisskopf is able to account for changes in the profit rate induced by changes in the utilization of productive capacity, the productivity of that capacity and shifts in the way in which income derived from production is distributed, and so the relationship between factor remuneration and factor productivity.[5]

Weisskopf's conclusions, drawn from his own empirical work for the non-financial corporate business (NFCB) sector of the US economy, are that the decline in the rate of profit on capital over the period 1949 to 1975 can be explained by a distributional shift away from profit income towards labour income. He also shows that labour pressure on profit share during each business upturn results in a premature peak in the rate of profit before the decline in real output. So the secular decline in the profit rate from cycle to cycle results from the cumulative effect of rising pressure on wage costs during this central phase of each cycle ('phase B') between the peak in profitability and peak in real output. In Chapter 6 we update and extend Weisskopf's work and arrive at a number of important qualifications to his conclusions for the USA. First, if one extends the period of analysis to include two further business cycles that occurred between 1975 and 1982 then the continued secular decline in American profitability appears to be explained by a progressive deterioration from cycle to cycle in the utilization of capacity. This is not surprising given the conditions of severe recession experienced by the American economy during this time. Second, if one decomposes labour share into the income shares of production staff, non-production staff and employer non-wage labour costs (primarily contributions to federal and private sector social insurance schemes) then it appears that the shift in distribution identified by Weisskopf that occurs over the secular period is the result of increase in the share of income being devoted to non-production staff and, particularly more recently, to non-wage labour costs.

Given the similarity that exists between the experience of profit rate decline in the USA and in the UK during the 1960s and 1970s (though the UK decline is not as severe as suggested by gross profit rate data (King 1975)) it is clearly a valuable exercise to perform a similar decomposition for the UK corporate sector. This task is attempted in Chapter 7. The principal result of this is that there exist a number of important differences between the American experience and that of the UK. Principally the secular decline in profitability in the UK is explained by a broader range of cumulative factors than those that explain the decline in the USA.

A METHODOLOGICAL FRAMEWORK

Weisskopf's profit rate decomposition

Weisskopf's approach proceeds from a decomposition of the rate of profit on capital into the three basic constituent components of the share of profits in income, the rate of capacity utilization, and the rate of potential capital productivity:

$$\frac{\Pi}{K} \equiv \frac{\Pi}{Y} \cdot \frac{Y}{Z} \cdot \frac{Z}{K} \equiv \sigma_\Pi \cdot U \cdot \theta \tag{5.1}$$

where Π is net profits, K is the net capital stock, Y is output and Z potential output.

Weisskopf argues that these three components of the rate of profit can be viewed as focusing on three different potential initial sources of profit rate decline. First, crises of technological change and rising organic composition of capital (in Marxian terminology) point to a decline in the rate of potential capital productivity as the source of the initial profit rate decline. Differential rates of growth of labour supply and capital supply lead to a falling relative price of capital. This in turn induces a change towards more capital-intensive production techniques. More capital is required for a particular potential level of output. With a given rate of capacity utilization and division of income between labour and capital the rate of profit must fall.[6]

Clearly the pattern of income distribution, expressed here as the share of profits, is of central importance in the explanation of the rate of profit. The second crisis variant encapsulated in equation 5.1 points to a declining profit share as the initial source of profit rate decline. The explanation for a falling profit share, Weisskopf suggests, is to be found in a changing balance of power between capital and labour in the competition over the distribution of income. Specifically, in Marxian terms, this might be explained by the 'reserve army' hypothesis, or in terms of growing trade union militancy and 'power'. This form of crisis parallels that discussed in general sociopolitical terms by Kalecki (1943), and we shall investigate this aspect further in Chapter 8. Weisskopf denotes this variant as 'rising strength of labour' crisis. It is, of course, a moot point whether a distributional shift towards labour is the result of reduced capital strength or increased labour strength. For example an increase in monopoly power, manifest in a larger overall mark-up and so larger profit share, can hardly be attributable to reduced labour strength. It is relative bargaining strength that is of importance. For this reason we refer to this variant more generally as 'distributional shift'.

Third, a profit rate decline may be precipitated by a fall in capacity utilization – 'realization failure'. The problem here is that some unforeseen reduction in aggregate demand prevents commodities being sold at profitable prices. Underconsumption theorists might point to an anticyclical or secularly declining share of wages in national income, working from the stylized 'fact' that the propensity to consume out of wage income is higher than that out of profit income (Bleaney 1976). Such a cyclical movement might arise as a result Hahnel and Sherman's 'wage-lag' hypothesis. Pitelis (1987) suggests that the enforced worker savings that have resulted from the pensions revolution in postwar USA and UK have sown the seeds of realization failure. Others point to the ability (Baran and Sweezy 1966) or inability (Nell 1988) of governments to maintain public spending at levels consistent with full employment as indicative of the ability or inability of the monopoly capitalist economy to avoid realization failure. Falling capacity utilization, from whatever source, will discourage further investment and so fuel the deterioration in aggregate demand conditions. In Chapter 2 we discussed direct links between growing monopolization of markets and declining capacity utilization.

However as the simple identity contained in equation 5.1 stands it is inadequate for analysing the effect of exogenous distributional changes (operating through the profit share component) on the rate of profit. This is because we must take account of the 'overhead-labour' effect. If capacity utilization falls then, because a proportion of the labour input is of an overhead nature and invariant to changes in the level of output, profit share will also fall. This observed fall in profit share cannot therefore be attributed to a shift in the balance of power between wage-earners and profit-earners, but is rather a concomitant effect of the fall in demand that generated the fall in utilization of capacity. This important point has been missed by many writers who have attempted to examine the behaviour of profitability over time, despite being pointed out as long ago as Steindl (1952). To account for this effect Weisskopf introduces the notion of a 'truly required' labour share, σ_w^*. If an enterprise suffers a fall in capacity utilization then it cannot immediately reduce capacity and overhead labour to short-run profit maximizing levels. Overhead labour is assumed to be employed in accordance with productive capacity. Actual labour share measures the labour share that results from actual employment of overhead labour. The truly required labour share measures the labour share that would be observed if overhead labour were employed in accordance with actual output.

$$\sigma_w^* = \frac{w_d L_d + w_o L_o^*}{Y} \qquad (5.2)$$

Where w_d and w_o are the wage rates of direct and overhead labour, L_d is employment of direct labour and L_o^* the truly required employment of overhead labour. The relationship between L_o^* and actual overhead labour employment is defined as follows:

$$L_o^* = (U \, / \, \hat{U}) \, L_o \qquad (5.3)$$

where U is the optimal level of capacity utilization, allowing some margin of planned excess capacity for strategic entry-deterrence purposes, future planned output expansion, etc. By dividing numerator and denominator of labour share through by L^* (the sum of L_d and L_0^*) we can then obtain values for truly required wage (w^*) and truly required labour productivity (y^*). It is possible to use appropriate wage good and output deflators to express these in real terms ($\bar{w}^*$ and $\bar{y}^*$) so:

$$\sigma_w^* = \frac{P_w}{P_y} \cdot \frac{\bar{w}^*}{\bar{y}^*} \tag{5.4}$$

The relationship between actual and truly required labour share that follows from this is given by:

$$\frac{\sigma_w^*}{\sigma_w} = \frac{W^*}{W} \equiv \epsilon_w \tag{5.5}$$

where W^* is the truly required total wage bill and W the actual total wage bill.

A similar decomposition to that in equation 5.4 can be applied to the rate of capital productivity, separating out the components of the real truly required capital–labour ratio ($\bar{j}^*$) and real truly required labour productivity from changes in the relative prices of capital goods and output.

$$\theta = \frac{P_y}{P_k} \cdot \frac{\bar{y}^*}{\bar{j}^*} \tag{5.6}$$

Returning to equation 5.1 we can decompose the growth rate of the profit rate in a growth-accounting identity as follows:

$$\dot{\Pi}/K = \dot{\sigma}_\Pi + \dot{U} + \dot{\theta} \tag{5.7}$$

where a dot above each variable denotes its exponential rate of change through time. Incorporating the decomposition of equations 5.2 to 5.5 equation 5.7 becomes:

$$\dot{\Pi}/K = -\Phi\,(\dot{\sigma}_w^* - \dot{\epsilon}_w) + \dot{U} + \dot{\Theta} \tag{5.8}$$

where Φ is a multiplier to convert the growth rate of the labour share into the growth rate of profit share. Since profit share and labour share are defined to sum to unity then:

$$\Phi = -\dot{\sigma}_\Pi\,/\,\dot{\sigma}_w \tag{5.9}$$

Separating equation 4.8 into adjusted contributions of capacity utilization changes and distributional shifts gives:

adjusted contribution of capacity utilization:

$$\dot{U}^* = \Phi\,\dot{\epsilon}_w + \dot{U} \tag{5.10}$$

adjusted contribution of distribution shift:

$$\dot{\sigma}_\Pi^* = -\Phi\,\dot{\sigma}_w^* = -\Phi\,(\dot{w}^* - \dot{y}^* + \dot{P}_w - \dot{P}_y) \tag{5.11}$$

contribution of capital productivity:

$$\dot{\Theta} = (\dot{y}^* - \dot{j}^*) + (\dot{P}_y - \dot{P}_k) \tag{5.12}$$

These three growth rate contributions sum to the growth rate of profit rate.

b) Further decomposition of labour share

In only going as far as decomposing income into profit and labour income Weisskopf's (1979) analysis conceals a great deal of information concerning the behaviour of different components of labour income and in particular the differences in the behaviour of wage and salary shares. Many political economists would regard the lumping together of wages and salaries into 'wage share' as an oversimplification since they may perform different roles in the process of production. For example Marx saw this distinction in terms of productive and unproductive labour, 'exploited' labour and the 'labour of exploiting'. As discussed in Chapter 2 in Kaleckian theories distribution is determined by the size of the mark-up on variable costs. The distinction is crucial since wages might be assumed to be a component of variable costs whereas salaries may be largely invariant to the level of output. Furthermore it might well be argued that wage-earners and salary-earners see themselves as distinctly different interest groups, the latter identifying themselves with the entrepreneurial class, or as a separate managerial class and so opposed to wage-earners in the distributional struggle (Zeitlin 1974, Baran and Sweezy 1966).

For the USA we are able to decompose labour income into the three components of 'wage' income (that paid to production staff), 'salary' income (that paid to non-production staff) and non-wage labour costs.[7] It is possible to perform a similar decomposition using UK data although in the UK the third component is only able to measure employers' labour tax (employers' national insurance contributions) and excludes contributions to private provision of health and pension insurance and other forms of deferred payment.

So equation 5.2 now becomes:

$$\sigma_w^{*\prime} = \frac{w_d^\prime L_d}{Y} + \frac{w_o^\prime L_o^*}{Y} + \frac{C^*}{Y} \tag{5.13}$$

where C^* is the truly required level of employers' non-wage labour costs and the wage rates $w_d^\prime$ and $w_o^\prime$ now exclude this non-wage component. C^* is computed as follows:

$$C^* = C_d + C_o^* \tag{5.14}$$

where C_d is the non-wage costs of production staff and C_o^* is the truly required level of non-wage costs of non-production staff. We assume the latter are employed according to the prevailing rate of capacity utilization. So:

$$C_o^* = (U / \hat{U}) C_o \tag{5.15}$$

To express the three shares in real terms we shall assume that all three components of labour income can be converted into real terms by the same wage–good price index. Therefore:

$$\sigma_w^{*\prime} = \frac{P_w}{P_y} \left[\frac{\overline{W}_d}{\overline{Y}} + \frac{\overline{W}_o^*}{\overline{Y}} + \frac{\overline{C}^*}{\overline{Y}} \right] \tag{5.16}$$

The transformation of equation 5.16 into a growth-accounting identity is not practicable since a change in one of the three component shares does not unambiguously imply a change in the same direction for total labour share (because the other components may also be changing) and hence a change in the opposite direction for profit share. Therefore we do not translate the rates of growth of these component shares into contributions to the growth rate of profit share using a multiplier.

In the two following chapters we present empirical evidence on the decomposition of profits outlined above for both the USA and the UK. The US evidence in part updates and extends that of Weisskopf (1979), making use in particular for the initial decomposition of the rate of profit new and revised estimates of the NFCB capital stock.

NOTES

1. See for example Glyn and Sutcliffe (1972), Panic and Close (1973), Burgess and Webb (1974), King (1975), Martin (1978).
2. See Nordhaus (1974), Schultze (1975) and Feldstein and Summers (1977).
3. For example Union of Radical Political Economists (1978), Wolff (1986), Michl (1989).
4. The overhead-labour hypothesis is also developed in Costrell (1981).
5. Weisskopf attributes changes in these components as evidence for various Marxian profitability crisis variants. However his method is clearly of general applicability to the explanation of profit rate behaviour.
6. Other variables may well change in response to this but for the purposes of identifying sources of the decline the rising organic composition crisis variant points to a declining potential capital productivity.
7. The terms 'wage' and 'salary' are used for expositional purposes and imply nothing about frequency of payment.

6. Income Shares and Profitability Crisis in the Postwar Period: Evidence for the USA

Weisskopf's original paper (Weisskopf 1979) reported results for the breakdown of the rate of profit explained in section 3(a) Chapter 5 for the non-financial corporate business (NFCB) sector of the US economy between 1949 and 1975. The non-financial corporate business sector accounts for approximately 60 per cent of American gross national product and covers all major private sector provision of goods and services, excluding financial activity. The period 1949–1975 covers five complete business cycles from trough to trough as consistent with US National Bureau of Economic Research dating.

Since the publication of Weisskopf's paper there have occurred two further complete business cycles in the US NFCB sector. These new cycles extend the quarterly data series to cover the period 1975 quarter 1 to 1982 quarter 4. These two cycles took place within general national and global conditions of deepening recession and rising unemployment. The first new cycle (cycle VI, if we continue Weisskopf's numbering) covers the period 1975 quarter 1 to 1980 quarter 2 with a peak in real output in 1979 quarter 1. The second additional cycle (cycle VII) is from 1980 quarter 2 to 1982 quarter 4 with a peak in real output in 1981 quarter 3. This cycle is very short, being curtailed sharply by the Reagan fiscal expansion,[1] but also deep as a result of monetary contraction. It has no late expansion phase since profit rate and real output peak simultaneously in 1981 quarter 3, and its expansion phase is very weak. NFCB real output at the close of this cycle stood at 654 billion 1972 dollars, somewhat below the level of real output at the close of the previous cycle. In addition we are able to include data for the initial expansion phase (phase A – see later) of an eighth cycle which we provisionally date as lasting from 1982 quarter 4 to 1985 quarter 3. Furthermore capital stock data for the US NFCB have been extensively revised[2] and so we present both revised and extended results for the period 1949 to 1985[3] (see Table 6.1).

Table 6.1   Rate of profit and real income in the US NFCB sector

Cycle	Phase	Quarter	$\overline{Y}$ \$ billion 1972 prices	Π/K per cent
		1949(4)	178.6	10.44
I	A			
		1950(4)	223.5	15.68
I	B			
		1953(2)	252.3	12.09
I	C			
		1954(2)	233.6	10.10
II	A			
		1955(2)	266.9	13.30
II	B			
		1957(1)	282.0	11.02
II	C			
		1958(2)	254.5	7.84
III	A			
		1959(2)	304.3	12.12
III	B			
		1960(1)	310.8	11.25
III	C			
		1960(4)	295.1	9.18
IV	A			
		1966(1)	431.3	14.62
IV	B			
		1969(2)	496.0	11.30
IV	C			
		1970(4)	472.0	7.86

Cycle	Phase	Quarter	$\bar{Y}$ $ billion	Π/K per cent
V	A			
		1972(4)	552.5	9.95
V	B			
		1973(3)	577.4	9.25
V	C			
		1975(1)	506.2	6.29
VI	A			
		1977(3)	644.7	9.63
VI	B			
		1979(1)	700.1	8.71
VI	C			
		1980(2)	667.2	6.68
VII	A			
		1981(3)	703.8	7.98
VII	C			
		1982(4)	653.5	5.62
VIII	A			
		1985(3)	815.6	9.68

Source: see Appendix to chapter.

In Weisskopf's original results the profit rate decline between 1949 and 1975 was attributable almost entirely to a decline in the share of profits in income. Only in the 1960s, when the rate of profit trended upwards (cycles III–IV), is the contribution of the change in profit share less important. This declining profit share Weisskopf identifies as indicative of rising strength of labour (the RSL variant). He goes on to show that labour pressure, as illustrated by various indicators of labour market 'tightness', on profit share during each business upturn results in a premature peak in the rate of profit before the decline in real output. He demonstrates that in each of the five complete business cycles that occurred between 1949 and 1975 a premature peak in the profit rate (in advance of the peak in real output) coincides with, and

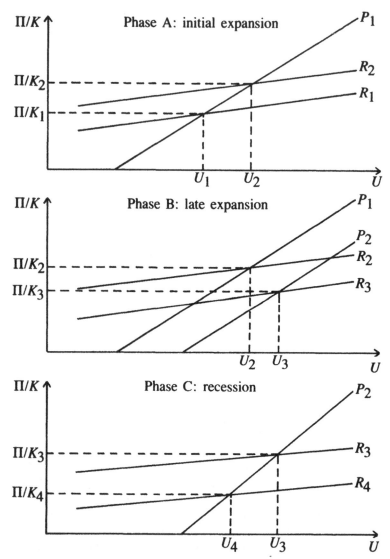

Figure 6.1   Potential and realizable profit in phases A, B and C of the business cycle

is precipitated by, a sharp increase in labour share. This increase is in turn the result of real wages starting to rise faster than real labour productivity. This period between the peak in profit rate and the subsequent peak in the level of real output Weisskopf terms the late expansion phase (numbered phase B). Figure 6.1 illustrates the basic features of each of the three phases of the cycle in terms of the model developed in Chapter 2. In phase A the growth in aggregate demand allows the realizable profit curve to shift upward so moving the system to a higher level of capacity utilization and improved rate of profit (U_2, Π/K_2). In phase B upward pressure on wage costs or perhaps the reduction in the degree of collusion between firms (Chapter 3) induces a downward movement in the potential profit curve. At the same time realizable profit begins to drop as the upswing runs out of steam but the combination of the two shifts allows a slightly higher capacity utilization but results in a reduction in the rate of profit (U_3, Π/K_3). In the final recession phase (phase C) the realizable profit curve shifts downwards as aggregate demand falls so causing a further reduction in the rate of profit and a downturn in capacity utilization (U_4, Π/K_4). So the secular decline in profit rate from cycle to cycle emerges out of the cumulative effect of rising labour pressure on wage costs during the critical late expansion phase of each cycle.

ACCOUNTING FOR CHANGES IN THE PROFIT RATE 1947–1985

Weisskopf's own results show that over the period 1949 to 1975 the rate of profit in the NFCB sector declined secularly on average at 1.2 per cent per annum. Table 6.2 shows the basic decomposition of changes in the rate of profit into changes in profit share, capacity utilization and capital productivity (equation 5.7). This shows that by extending his data into the 1980s the overall decline in the rate of profit worsens to 1.7 per cent per annum if one measures the trend from the beginning of cycle I to the end of cycle VII. If we take the trend from the profit rate peak in cycle I to the profit rate peak in cycle VIII (the end of phase VIIIA) then the decline is slightly less severe at 1.55 per cent per annum. Table 6.2 also shows that on the basis of the simple decomposition of profit rate

Table 6.2   Simple decomposition of changes in the rate of profit: US NFCB sector

	Average annual exponential percentage rates of growth			
	$\dot{\Pi}/K$	$\dot{\sigma}_\Pi$	$\dot{U}$	$\dot{\theta}$
Phase averages[1]				
A	22.94	15.52	7.63	−0.22
B	−7.93	−6.86	0.58	−1.66
C	−24.50	−15.69	−10.39	1.58
Between cycles[2]				
I–II	−3.09	−2.14	−0.29	−0.66
II–III	−2.04	−1.31	−1.35	0.63
III–IV	2.38	0.81	0.97	0.60
IV–V	−4.58	−3.29	−0.45	−0.84
V–VI	−0.57	1.06	−0.17	−1.46
VI–VII	−4.98	−3.27	−1.83	0.12
Full period[3]				
IA to VIIC	−1.69	−1.20	−0.17	−0.32
IB to VIIIA	−1.55	−1.02	0.23	−0.30

Source: see Appendix to chapter.
Notes:
1. The growth rate for each variable in each phase is computed as 100 x (log $x(t_2)$ − log $x(t_1)$) / (t_2 − t_1), where $x(t_1)$ and $x(t_2)$ refer to values at the start and end of a phase, and $t_2 − t_1$ is the length of phase in years. Phase averages are calculated as simple averages of these individual phase growth rates.

2. Computed as above but $x(t_1)$ and $x(t_2)$ are in this case geometric means of the variables for each cycle and are ascribed to the mid-point of the cycle, and $t_2 − t_1$ measures the time between these mid-points in years.

3. Obtained by estimating an ordinary least squares regression of log (x) on a constant and time (measured in years), and multiplying the slope coefficient from this regression by 100.

by far the main part of this decline is the result of a decline in profit share. The other two variables appear to contribute little to the decline, and indeed if the trend is measured from phase IB to phase VIIIC the slight upward trend in capacity utilization acts against the profit rate decline. The improvement in profitability in the mid-1960s (cycles III–IV) is also clearly apparent. It appears to be due to roughly equal improvements in all three components. The results for the period after 1975 show that initially (cycles V–VI) the decline in profitability is slight, largely because of a significant improvement in profit share (of over 1 per cent per annum) working against in particular declining capital productivity. However from 1980 to 1982 (cycles VI–VIII) the aggregate profit rate plummets at nearly 5 per cent per annum. This is composed of a unprecedentedly sharp decline in capacity utilization, precipitated by the deflationary economic policies of the newly elected Reagan administration, and a rapid decline in profit share. The premature peak in profitability highlighted by Weisskopf can be seen in the phase average figures contained in the same table. Although capacity utilization continues to make slight improvement during phase B, the profit rate starts to decline as profit share falls.

In Table 6.3 results are presented for the more elaborate decomposition of the rate of profit, taking into account the 'overhead-labour' effect (equations 5.10 to 5.12). What emerges from the trend results is that realization conditions (adjusted capacity utilization) are now of considerably greater importance in accounting for the secular decline in profitability. If the trend is measured from phase IA to phase VIIC then distribution conditions (adjusted profit share) and realization conditions contribute in roughly similar proportions to the profit rate decline. If the trend is measured from phase IB to phase VIIIA then realization conditions are now of greater importance, contributing almost 0.8 per cent points to the 1.55 per cent decline in the profit rate. Differences also emerge from the between-cycle decomposition. Realization conditions now become considerably more important in accounting for each between-cycle movement in the rate of profit. Profitability growth in the 1960s is now largely accounted for by the sustained improvement in capacity utilization, leading to improved utilization of overhead labour. The two most

Table 6.3   Decomposition of changes in the rate of profit with adjustment for under-utilization of labour: US NFCB sector

	Average annual exponential percentage rates of growth			
	Π/K	$\dot{\sigma}_\Pi^*$	$\dot{U}^*$	$\dot{\theta}$
Phase averages				
A	22.94	5.94	17.22	−0.22
B	−7.93	−7.59	1.32	−1.66
C	−24.50	2.03	−28.11	1.58
Between cycles				
I–II	−3.09	−1.62	−0.81	−0.66
II–III	−2.04	0.55	−3.22	0.63
III–IV	2.38	−0.25	2.03	0.60
IV–V	−4.58	−2.56	−1.18	−0.84
V–VI	−0.57	1.60	−0.71	−1.46
VI–VII	−4.98	1.28	−6.38	0.12
Full period				
IA to VIIC	−1.69	−0.75	−0.62	−0.32
IB to VIIIA	−1.55	−0.46	−0.79	−0.30

Source: see Appendix to chapter.
Notes: see Table 6.2.

recent between-cycle decompositions also show considerable changes from Table 6.2. From cycles V to VI we observe a marked 'improvement' in distributional conditions, which would have *ceteris paribus* led to a 1.6 per cent annum growth in the rate of profit in the late 1970s results from declining capacity utilization and declining capital productivity, although the latter is still of greater importance. The improvement in distributional conditions now carries over into the 1980–1982 period (cycles VI–VII).

Worsening realization conditions are now seen to account entirely for the very sharp decline in the profit rate. The phase average growth rates also highlight the fact that once account is taken of the overhead-labour effect realization conditions form the main contribution to the initial growth in the profit rate in phase A, and to the decline in phase C. However in phase B it is still clear that distributional pressure is responsible for the premature cyclical profit rate downturn.

Table 6.4 Breakdown of changes in capital productivity and adjusted profit share in the US NFCB sector

	Average annual exponential percentage rates of growth				
	1	2	3	4	5
Adjusted profit share	$\dot{\sigma}_\Pi^*$	$-\Phi\dot{\sigma}_w$	$\Phi\dot{w}$	$\Phi\dot{y}$	$-\Phi(\dot{P}_w - \dot{P}_y)$
Phase averages					
A	5.94	6.23	−13.82	20.05	−0.29
B	−7.59	−4.78	−8.88	4.11	−2.82
C	2.03	4.64	−0.42	5.05	−2.60
Between cycles					
I–II	−1.62	−3.25	−14.83	11.57	1.63
II–III	0.55	1.29	−9.99	11.28	−0.74
III–IV	−0.25	0.45	−11.19	11.63	−0.70
IV–V	−2.56	0.71	−10.18	9.47	−1.85
V–VI	1.60	4.34	−2.54	6.88	−2.74
VI–VIII	1.28	9.85	0.71	9.15	−8.57
Full period					
IA to VIIC	−0.75	0.73	−9.97	10.70	−1.48
IB to VIIIA	−0.46	1.37	−8.90	10.27	−1.83

	Average annual exponential percentage rates of growth			
	1	2	3	4
Capital productivity	$\dot{\theta}$	$\dot{y}^*$	$\dot{j}^*$	$\dot{P}_y - \dot{P}_k$
Phase averages				
A	−0.22	4.63	4.20	−0.64
B	−1.66	1.04	1.28	−1.42
C	1.58	1.01	0.92	1.49
Between cycles				
I–II	−0.66	3.09	3.16	−0.59
II–III	0.63	2.88	1.27	−0.98
III–IV	0.60	3.02	2.46	0.04
IV–V	−0.84	2.07	2.03	−0.89
V–VI	−1.46	1.31	1.28	−1.49
VI–VII	0.12	1.85	2.66	0.93
Full period				
IA to VIIC	−0.32	2.44	2.13	−0.63
IB to VIIIA	−0.30	2.33	2.08	−0.55

Source: see Appendix to chapter.
Notes: see Table 6.2.

Table 6.4 provides the further breakdown of movements in distributional conditions (adjusted profit rate) in equation 5.11, and in capital productivity in equation 5.12. For adjusted profit share columns 3 and 4 give the contributions of real truly required hourly labour compensation and real productivity growth. Each is multiplied by the multiplier Φ to provide a percentage point contribution. So for example from column 3 we see that averaged across the cycles the rise in the real truly required wage rate in phase A would contribute, *ceteris paribus*, a 13.82 percentage point fall in the rate of profit. These two columns add together to give column 2 the contribution of the real truly required labour share. When this is added to the contribution of relative price changes in column 5 the overall change in adjusted profit share in column 1 is obtained. For capital productivity changes in the second half of the table column 1 gives the overall growth rate, columns 2 and 3 the growth rates of real truly required labour productivity and the real truly required capital–labour ratio, and column 4 the contribution of relative price changes. As shown in equation 5.12 column 1 therefore equals column 2 minus column 3 plus column 4.

The intra-cycle average figures show that the contribution of productivity changes dominates that of real wage changes except in phase B. This result is also supported by Hahnel and Sherman (1982a, 1982b) in their empirical analysis. Price effects are relatively important. In the important late expansion phase, phase B, the decline in the real wage share occurs because real wage growth, despite slowing down, does not slow down as much as real productivity. The between-cycle decomposition shows that the improvement in distributional conditions in the late 1970s and 1980s arises because of the pronounced slowdown in real wage growth. In fact from cycles VI to VII real wages fall. This means that productivity growth outstrips real wage growth quite considerably particularly in the last between-cycle period. However these figures also reveal up to cycle VI the progressive deterioration in productivity growth rates. This corroborates with the results of Wolff (1986) and Michl (1989) who attribute the profits squeeze of the 1960s and early 1970s as mainly the result of a productivity slowdown. Over the full period we observe that real wage growth provides a 9 or 10 percentage point per annum contribution to the fall in the profit rate. However this is just outpaced by the trend contribution from the growth in real productivity. The deterioration in distributional conditions results from adverse price movements working against the resultant decline in real labour share. In his original paper Weisskopf denoted this effect 'defensive labour strength', an improvement 'in the value of output in terms of its ability to meet worker's consumption needs' (Weisskopf 1979, p. 357). However it is clear that the origins of such relative price movements may have nothing to do with the actions of workers and so the terminology may be misleading (Munley 1981, Weisskopf 1981). Adverse price movements also provide the major contribution to the secular decline in capital productivity, particularly in the 1970s (between cycles V and VI). Michl (1989) also attributes much of the decline in capital productivity to adverse price movements.

ACCOUNTING FOR THE COMPOSITION OF AGGREGATE LABOUR SHARE

In this section the share of employee compensation in domestic income is decomposed into three smaller shares. Following the methodology outlined in Chapter 5 we distinguish between wage share, salary share and supplemental labour cost share. This last component measures the share of employer contributions to federal old age and unemployment insurance programmes and to voluntary health, unemployment and pension schemes and stock purchase schemes.

Figure 6.2 shows the behaviour of these shares for the NFCB sector in the postwar period. The share of production worker wages falls from 57 per cent of net income in 1948 to 40 per cent in 1983 while salary share in the same period rises from 17 per cent to over 30 per cent, and the share of supplemental labour costs from 4 per cent of net income to 14 per cent. *Prima facie*, this suggests that production workers as a group have lost out in distributional terms, to the advantage of non-production staff. However two qualifications must follow this. First (Figure 6.2), production workers as a proportion of the total have steadily declined in the postwar period from above 80 per cent of total employment to around or below 70 per cent. Second, we must note that some proportion of the rising share of pensions, health and unemployment insurance contributions would have been paid on behalf of production workers and so would have offset the downward trend in production workers' payroll share.

We now consider actual growth rates of the three component shares for the postwar period. Between-cycle average growth rates for employee compensation share and the three component shares are presented in Table 6.5.[4]

Real truly required employee compensation share fell in four out of six of the cycle-to-cycle periods, particularly between cycles II and III in the late 1950s, and between V and VI, and VI and VII from 1975 to 1982. However during the long boom from the

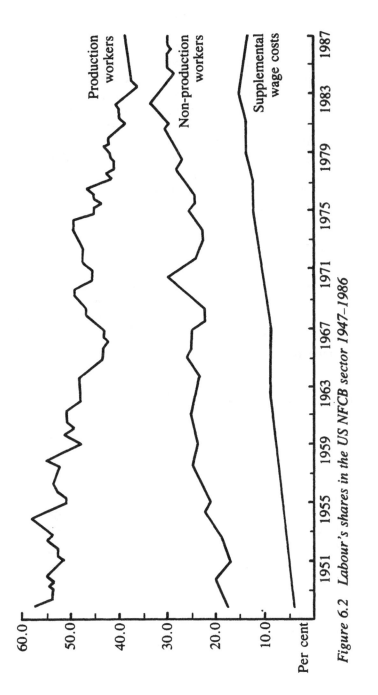

Figure 6.2   Labour's shares in the US NFCB sector 1947–1986

1960s to the early 1970s (cycles IV to V) when labour markets were generally 'tight' the trend is an upward one. However during this period particularly identified by Boddy and Crotty (1975) as exemplifying the rising labour strength phenomenon, despite an overall growth in the truly required labour share both wage and salary share decline. The upward trend in the aggregate share is accounted for by a rapidly increasing share of truly required supplemental labour cost. Between cycles IV and V this share rose at nearly 3.7 per cent per annum on average (only in the early 1950s, between cycles I and II, was this rate exceeded when the level of the share was at a very low base).

Table 6.5   Composition of labour share in the US NFCB sector

Changes in unadjusted components	Average annual exponential percentage rates of growth			
	1	2	3	4
	σ_w	W_d/Y	W_o/Y	C/Y
Phase averages				
A	−3.59	−4.26	−3.53	0.30
B	1.74	1.21	1.76	4.78
C	3.13	0.29	7.18	6.32
Between cycles				
I–II	0.57	−0.77	3.05	4.19
II–III	0.34	−1.29	2.94	3.99
III–IV	−0.21	−1.10	0.69	2.44
IV–V	0.72	0.33	0.16	4.24
V–VI	−0.20	−2.04	1.14	3.76
VI–VII	0.66	−1.93	3.84	1.95
Full period				
IA to VIIC	0.27	−0.85	1.28	3.58
IB to VIIIA	0.23	−0.96	1.29	3.38

	Average annual exponential percentage rates of growth			
Changes in truly required shares:	1	2	3	4
	$\sigma_w^{*\,\prime}$	$\overline{W}_d/\overline{Y}$	$\overline{W}_o^{*}/\overline{Y}$	$\overline{C}^{*}/\overline{Y}$
Phase averages				
A	−1.44	−4.43	4.03	2.45
B	1.22	0.49	1.63	4.26
C	−0.92	−0.23	−2.20	2.27
Between cycles				
I–II	0.87	−0.34	3.20	4.49
II–III	−0.33	−1.48	1.40	3.33
III–IV	−0.12	−1.29	1.47	2.54
IV–V	0.16	−0.08	−0.70	3.68
V–VI	−0.83	−2.56	0.45	3.14
VI–VII	−1.99	−3.67	0.27	−0.71
Full period				
IA to VIIC	−0.17	−1.18	0.77	3.14
IB to VIIIA	−0.31	−1.38	0.64	2.84

Source: see Appendix to chapter.
Notes: see Table 6.2.

Real production worker wage share shows a downward trend in each cycle-to-cycle period – overall a downward postwar trend of 1 per cent per annum. The conclusion here is very strong, that production workers have consistently as a group lost ground throughout the postwar period and have at no time been able to restore the progressive redistribution of income away from them. Data on the changes in the relative sizes of the production and salaried workforces offer some explanation for this (Figure 6.2), although to appeal to the explanation of changing employment composition fails to account for why this change has taken place. Real truly required salary share shows an upward trend in the first three cycle-to-cycle periods, until the early 1960s, but after cycle

III this trend too becomes a downward one. This suggests that although actual salary share has risen steadily through the postwar period (Figure 6.2) this rise can, after the peak in capacity utilization in the early 1960s, be explained by the effect of falling levels of capacity utilization and consequent under-utilization of overhead labour. With the steadily worsening economic conditions in the 1970s American capitalists found their overhead labour costs rising proportionate to other costs as their overhead labour inputs have been geared to capacity output levels increasingly above actual production levels. In the last two cycle-to-cycle periods, from 1975 to 1982, production workers' real wage share has fallen at an average rate of over 2 per cent per annum, faster than at any other time since 1949. The trend of real truly required salary, although falling, is at a slower rate.

Real truly required supplemental labour cost share, in contrast to the other two components, has shown consistent and relatively rapid growth throughout the postwar period, until the last cycle-to-cycle period (VI–VII). So although all workers, and in particular production workers, have failed to maintain their real income shares, this has been in part made up by increasing non-wage benefits. These non-wage benefits essentially comprise 'deferred' wages since workers receive this form of remuneration at some point in the future if or when they become ill, unemployed, or retired. In the case of the compulsory portion of these payments the initial recipient is the federal government. However for the voluntary schemes control is vested in private trustees. In the case of the largest component of these, pension schemes, a series of postwar legislation stemming from the 1947 Taft–Hartley Act ensures that schemes are operated and controlled by the financial capital sector, divorced from individual member ownership (Barber and Rifkin 1978). Freeman and Medoff (1984) show that unionized establishments, *ceteris paribus*, pay 30 per cent higher fringe benefit expenditures, suggesting that where union organization is strong and workers are able to express preferences more effectively, those preferences are weighted towards fringe benefits. In the context of the American coal industry Farber (1978) shows that union members value a dollar of fringe benefits almost 40 per cent more than a dollar of pre-tax pay. An explanation for this may be found in the tax advantage to be gained from payment in fringe benefits. So although workers may have a preference for fringe benefits this preference may be reinforced by the desires of capital. Pension schemes, in particular, may promote worker attachment and reduce wage cost variability, especially if pension portability is restricted (Becker 1964, Green 1982). Finally the massive reserves of funds now held by pension funds in the developed capitalist world provide an essential source of general investment funds (Minns 1980, Barber and Rifkin 1978). Pitelis (1987) goes as far as to argue that these reserves may have led to 'over-saving', with resulting detrimental consequences for profit realization.

Also contained in Table 6.5 are the rates of growth of real truly required employee compensation share and the three components within each cycle phase. These average figures for each phase show that it is in phase B of each cycle that production workers can make real wage share gains, but these gains disappear over the secular trend. So for production workers Weisskopf's conclusion that it is in the late expansion phase between profit rate peak and real output peak that tight labour market conditions allow real wage increases is supported. This is strengthened by the fact that real truly required supplemental labour cost share, although rising on average in all phases of the cycles, rises fastest in phase B. We can note that because cycle VII has no phase B, production workers fared particularly badly in the early 1980s. In the downturn of cycle VII their real wage share bears the distributional brunt of the 1982 recession by falling at an unprecedented 9 per cent per annum. The sharp slump in the American economy engineered by the newly elected Reagan administration after 1980 seems to have brought about a sharp redistribution of income away from production workers towards salaried workers. Real truly required salary share rose at over 8 per cent per annum in phase VIIC. The figure here is adjusted for the utilization effect so this sharp decline cannot be explained in terms of differential rates of adjustment between direct and overhead labour inputs.

The cyclical pattern of real truly required salary share is quite different from that of production wage share. Real salary share rises fastest during phase A of each cycle, levels off in phase B and declines in phase C. So the cyclical pattern of salary share conforms closely to that of profit share, and contrasts with the clear inverse relationship between wage share and profit share.

In the long business cycle of the 1960s (cycle IV) the direction of salary share changes corresponds precisely to the direction of profit rate and profit share changes. Certainly during the 1960s, and to a lesser extent in other periods since 1949, when profit share has risen so has the income share of non-production workers.

Moseley (1985) suggests that declining profit rate can be explained by the rising proportion of overhead labour, since proportionately less 'productive' labour is being employed to generate capitalist surplus. This may be correct in so far as this rising proportion of overhead labour is indicative of the secular worsening of realization conditions (especially since the postwar capacity utilization peak in 1964), and so under-utilization of overhead labour. However if we control for this effect then we find there exists a positive relationship between profit rate and the size of the truly required salaried workforce. At a given level of utilization of productive capacity the distributional balance is between on the one hand profits and salaries and on the other the wages of direct production staff. This pattern is consistent with the development of managerialism, and certainly is suggestive of the need of large corporations to absorb rising profits into discretionary managerial expenditures (Baran and Sweezy 1966, Cowling 1982). It may also be indicative of continued growth in the army of administrative and technical staff required to maintain and improve managerial control over the production process (Braverman 1974).

WAGE SHARE AND THE DEGREE OF MONOPOLY IN AMERICAN MANUFACTURING

Having discovered that the trend of wage share has since the Second World War been markedly different from the trend of salary share and from the trend of overall employee compensation share, the question of what determines that wage share trend remains. In this section we explore the applicability of the Kaleckian idea that wage share is determined by the structural characteristics of final product markets within the economy.

The literature on changing patterns of concentration in the postwar American economy provides only sparse evidence to suggest that the secular decline in wage share can be explained by rising concentration. White (1981) concludes that there is little evidence of an upward trend in aggregate concentration. Scherer (1980) states that if any increase has occurred it has been at a pace of no more than 'glacial drift'. He also finds evidence of only a slowly rising trend of average market concentration. Shepherd (1982), examining shares of national income generated by industries within different concentration bands, concludes that competition in the American economy has increased significantly in the years between 1939 and 1980. Most of the change has occurred since 1958.

Concentration is only one aspect of monopoly power; for example it cannot capture changes in the pattern of collusion within oligopolistic industries. Furthermore it may only bear an incomplete relationship to the welfare implications of monopolization. Gordon (1985) examines postwar changes in performance measures of monopoly power in the USA and argues, from observing the secular growth in Tobin's 'q' and the Lerner index, that monopoly power increased sharply from the end of the Second World War until the early 1970s. In the mid-1970s these declined and he suggests that this was due to rising foreign competition.

Figure 6.3 shows the behaviour of the margin of revenue over direct costs, and equivalent to k in equation 2.7 for the post-war period. From 1947 until 1971 the series shows a significant upward trend. The margin of shipments over direct costs as a percentage of shipments rises from 23.7 per cent in 1947 to almost 33 per cent in 1971. Table 6.6 shows the behaviour of each of the three variables in equation 2.7. In the same period production wage share falls from over forty per cent to thirty per cent of value added, but the ratio of materials bill to production wage bill (j in equation 2.7) remains largely constant. After the peak in 1971 the aggregate revenue-cost margin series falls, levelling off in the mid and late 1970s at around 31 per cent. It then starts to rise again in the 1980s. On the other hand wage share continues to decline throughout the 1970s and early 1980s, and the *j* ratio rises.

There are several possible explanations for the upward trend of the margin of revenue over direct cost. First a secular trend towards higher average levels of vertical integration at the establishment level would cause its value to rise. However it seems

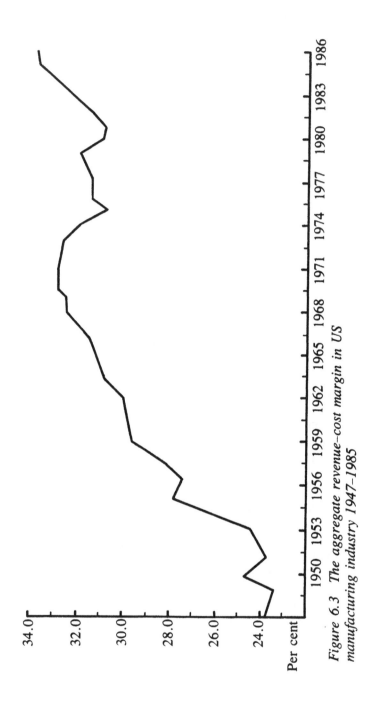

Figure 6.3   The aggregate revenue–cost margin in US manufacturing industry 1947–1985

Table 6.6 US manufacturing: production wage share, the aggregate revenue–cost margin and ratio of wages to materials 1947–1985

Averages	Production worker wage share of value added (per cent)	Revenue–cost margin[1] (per cent)	Ratio of materials bill to production[2] wage bill
1947	40.7	23.7	3.69
1949–51	39.5	23.9	3.88
1952–54	39.5	24.8	3.65
1955–57	36.0	27.5	3.69
1958–60	34.3	28.8	3.72
1961–63	32.0	30.0	3.74
1964–66	31.5	31.3	3.74
1967–69	30.8	32.3	3.66
1970–72	30.0	32.9	3.77
1973–75	28.1	31.9	4.55
1976–78	26.9	31.5	4.97
1979–81	25.6	31.4	5.45
1982–84	24.2	32.5	5.53
1985	23.6	33.5	5.41

1 Computed as (value added minus production wages)/value of shipments.
2 For 1947–57 computed as (value of shipments minus value added)/production wages

Sources: Value of shipments 1947–57: US Department of Commerce, *Manufacturers' shipments, Inventories and Orders* (1963). All other series: US Department of Commerce, *Annual Survey of Manufactures* (various years)

unlikely that this explanation could account for all the sustained upward trend through the 1950s and 1960s. The increase in vertical integration would have needed to have been of a very large order, and to have been achieved without problems of diseconomies of scale and loss of managerial control. A second explanation would be that firms have over time found themselves bearing a greater proportion of costs as overheads. In this case the profit margin as measured here will rise. Most of the changing composition of employment from production to overhead staff, after allowing for the effect of changing capacity utilization, occurred in the 1950s. Between 1947 and 1959 truly required salaried staff as a percentage of the truly required total rose from 15 per cent to 25 per cent. However in the later 1960s and 1970s the change that did occur is largely explained by falling capacity utilization, since truly required salaried staff as a percentage of the truly required total remains fairly constant. A third explanation is the Kaleckian idea that a rising revenue–direct cost margin is linked to rising monopoly power. If this explanation is to hold then it appears most plausible in the 1960s. Although market concentration figures for the 1960s do not show large increases (Scherer 1980, Mueller and Hamm 1974), writers such as Cowling (1982) would argue that a rising internationalization of production and high levels of conglomerate and horizontal merger activity during the 1960s resulted in a concentration of market power both within and across markets, and in the monopsonistic power of large corporations in factor markets.

After 1971 the impact of rising materials costs, the result of large increases in world energy prices, is captured dramatically by the increase in the j ratio. At the same time American markets started to experience sharply rising levels of import penetration. The monopoly capital thesis of a tendency for the degree of monopoly to rise breaks down in the face of rising competition (Auerbach and Skott 1988). The drop in the revenue–direct cost margin suggests that American manufacturers were unable wholly to pass increased energy costs on into final prices, and that increased foreign competition further reduced the extent to which prices could be set above marginal costs. The trend of wage share throughout the 1970s remains downward. The data point to a continued decline in production worker wage share in the early 1980s, and a sharp rise in the margin of revenue over direct costs towards the pre-OPEC price rise peak level (Figure 6.3). The most plausible explanation for this widening wedge between revenue and direct cost is in a declining strength of production labour argument, the result of sharper competition in labour markets in conditions of unemployment and recession. Table 6.5 shows that between cycles VI and VII real production wage share fell sharply, suggesting that in the early 1980s production workers were unable to secure wage bargains to maintain real wage levels, or that employers were able to achieve a productivity breakthrough. As discussed earlier the data in Table 6.5 show that the reduction in real production wage share in phase VIIC coincides with a progressive rise in real salary share. So the early 1980s experience points to a rise in the revenue–direct cost margin resulting from a decline in production worker strength and redistribution towards salaried workers, rather than any independently observable increase in the monopoly power of American manufacturing industry.

CONCLUSIONS

One of the most important conclusions to emerge from this chapter concerning the behaviour of aggregate profitability is the importance of the relative size of real wage and real productivity growth rates. To risk making too much of a tautology movements in profit and aggregate labour share depend on these quantities. Our results find considerable support for productivity slowdown as an explanation for the decline in profitability in the early 1960s and early 1970s. From 1975 onwards the slowdown in productivity growth is certainly not reversed to any degree, and yet it becomes less important as a contributory factor towards the sustained poor profit performance of the American economy because of the very pronounced slowdown in real wage growth. And so from 1975, along with Michl (1989), we can identify a second stage in the aggregate profitability decline during which other explanations become important. From 1975 to 1980 our results point to the effect of adverse price movements on capital productivity, as the price of capital goods outpaces that of output. In the early 1980s the dominant influence is unequivocably the chronic rise in excess capacity.

In his original paper Weisskopf (1979) concluded that the rising strength of labour variant received far more empirical support than other explanations of profit rate decline in the USA. This chapter has brought two qualifications to this conclusion. First, with the addition of two subsequent cycles from 1975 to 1982 we have found that during these seven years all the secular decline in the rate of profit is explained by a deterioration in realization conditions, indicative of the chronic excess capacity of the early 1980s. In fact this deterioration was so sharp that over the full postwar period we find that distribution and realization conditions now contribute in equal proportions to the overall postwar decline in the rate of profit.

Second, our decomposition of labour share has shown that different components of labour income have experienced markedly different secular and cyclical behaviour. Real production worker wage share has displayed a cyclical behaviour inversely related to profit share around a consistent downward trend. In contrast real salary share shows a pro-cyclical behaviour, closely matched to that of profit share. Until the early 1960s it shows an upward trend, but after then, when adjusted for the effect of changing capacity utilization on the use of overhead labour, it starts to decline. Actual salary share rises consistently throughout the postwar period. The share of supplemental labour cost rises both secularly and within each phase of the cycle. We have explored a number of explanations for the different patterns of each of these three components. First, it is apparent that the secular worsening of labour strength conditions identified by Weisskopf is largely explained by the increasing share of income devoted to 'deferred' wages, principally pension, health and unemployment insurance contributions. Questions of whether workers have reluctantly or willingly accepted this growth in fringe benefits, and whether these payments are in addition to 'take-home' pay or comprise a second-best alternative to unattainable rising real wages remains. However it does seem likely that this growth coincides with the desires of capital. Second, the changing composition of employment, away from production workers towards overhead staff, is an important explanatory factor. However the question of why, net of the effect of increasing under-utilization of overhead labour, this change has taken place, also remains. We tentatively suggest that it may indicate rising administrative and technical control over the production process, and more generally the growth of managerialism. Third, we have sought to identify the growth of monopoly power in the American economy with the apparent upward movement of the margin of price over direct unit cost, as an explanatory factor for declining production wage share. If this does provide an explanation for distributional trends it seems likely that as such its applicability is limited to the 1960s.

APPENDIX

Data sources and definitions

All data series are seasonally adjusted quarterly series unless otherwise indicated.

The data definitions used in the decomposition of the rate of profit correspond exactly to those used by Weisskopf (1979) (see Appendix, pp. 377–378). All the series have been extended to 1985 quarter 3 and where extensive revisions have been made since 1979 in the published series (as for example with the capital stock data) these revised series have been used.

Π Net pre-tax profits of the NFCB sector, current prices. This is the sum of 'corporate profits with inventory valuation adjustment and capital consumption adjustment' and 'net interest' (*source* NIPA).

$K,\overline{K}$ Total net capital stock at current and constant prices. This is obtained from annual end-year data on residential and non-residential net fixed capital in the NFCB sector, in current and 1972 prices (*source* SCB). Mid-year values were interpolated and added to these were mid-year estimates of inventories in the NFCB sector (*source* Holland and Myers 1979). Constant price values of inventories were obtained by using as a deflator the US Department of Labor wholesale price index for industrial commodities. Post-1979 mid-year inventory data were approximated on the basis of second quarter data for non-farm inventories (*source* SCB), available in both constant and current prices. The resulting mid-year estimates of total net capital were converted to quarterly data by linear interpolation.

$Y, \bar{Y}$ Net income in current and constant prices.
NFCB net income in current and 1972 prices (*source* NIPA). Definitionally this is equal to Π plus W.

W Total employee compensation.
'Compensation of employees' in the NFCB sector in current prices (*source* NIPA).

Z Capacity net income.
This was computed as NFCB net income divided by the Federal Reserve Board rate of capacity utilization for manufacturing (*source* FRB). The resulting series was then smoothed using a centred seven-quarter moving average.

U Capacity utilization.
The series for capacity utilization used in the analysis was computed as net income divided by capacity net income (after smoothing).

$\hat{U}$ Optimal capacity utilization.
This is set at 90 per cent, since the actual capacity utilization series only on one occasion exceeds this figure, and then by a very small margin.

L Total labour hours.
This is obtained by multiplying an index of total labour hours in the NFCB sector (1967 = 100) (*source* MLR) by an estimate of actual total hours for 1967 obtained from Gorman (1972).

$w_d L_d$ Production staff wage bill (wage x employment).

$w_o L_o$ Non-production staff wage bill.
It is not possible to obtain this breakdown of W and L for the NFCB sector directly so the two series were apportioned between direct and overhead labour using linearly interpolated annual data for manufacturing on production worker wage bill, non-production worker wage bill, production worker total man-hours, and non-

production employment (*source* ASM/COM). Non-production total hours was estimated as 2000 hours per employee per annum.

P_y Output price deflator, 1972 = 100
Simply computed as the implicit deflator for NFCB net income.

P_w Wage good price deflator, 1972 = 100.
The series used here is the US Department of Labor's monthly consumer price index for all items (1967 = 100), converted to a quarterly series, keyed to 1972, and seasonally adjusted using an arithmetic moving average.

P_k Capital good price index, 1972 = 100.
The implicit deflator for our capital stock series was used.

j^* Real truly required capital–labour ratio.
Computed as real capital stock divided by truly required employment, L^*.

For the decomposition of labour share into its three components the total wage and salary bill for the NFCB sector is taken as 'compensation of employees' minus 'supplements to wages and salaries', and was then allocated to production and non-production staff as above.

C Non-wage and salary labour costs.
'Supplements to wages and salaries' in the NFCB sector (*source* NIPA).

C_d, C_o Production and non-production non-wage labour costs. No direct breakdown is obtainable so these were apportioned according to the proportion of production and non-production wage costs in the total wage and salary bill. So:

$$C_d = W_d / (W_d + W_o) \cdot C \text{ and}$$
$$C_o = W_o / W_d + W_o) \cdot C$$

Abbreviations

ASM *Annual Survey of Manufactures*, US Bureau of the Census
COM *Census of Manufactures*, US Bureau of the Census
FRB *Federal Reserve Bulletin*, Federal Reseerve Board of the United States
MLR *Monthly Labor Review*, US Department of Labor
NIPA *National Income and Product Accounts*, US Department of Commerce
SCB *Survey of Current Business*, US Department of Commerce

NOTES

1. Cycle VII does, however, conform to the NBER business cycle definition (see Weisskopf 1979, footnote p. 350).
2. Substantially revised estimates of gross fixed reproducible tangible wealth in the USA for the period 1925 to 1982 were reported in *Survey of Current Business*, US Department of Commerce, Volume 66, No. 1, January 1986. Data for the subsequent period are reported in various subsequent issues.
3. An earlier version of some of the empirical work reported in this chapter, which did not take account of the revised NFCB sector capital stock data, was reported in Henley (1987b).
4. An idea of the importance of the rates of change of each share in explaining the rate of change of profit share can be gained by considering the levels of each real truly required income share (Figure 5.2).

7. Income Shares and Profitability Crisis in the Postwar Period: Evidence for the UK

ACCOUNTING FOR CHANGES IN THE PROFIT RATE IN THE UK 1962–1985

In this chapter we present a similar empirical breakdown for UK aggregate profitability on a quarterly basis to that in Chapter 6 for the USA, using the methodology of Chapter 5.[1] The profit measure used refers to the profits of UK industrial and commercial companies (ICCs).[2] These data provide the closest available approximation to a definition of UK non-financial corporate private sector business enterprise, and so are virtually equivalent to the NFCB sector analysed for the USA in the previous chapter. The profit measure used is a net pre-tax measure of gross corporate income, i.e. it includes rent and other income from non-trading activities and is after deduction for capital consumption and stock appreciation. It thus attempts to provide as close as possible a measure to the net flow of corporate income generated from the corporate private sector capital stock, that which Nordhaus (1974) terms 'genuine capital income'. The definition and source of profit and other series used in the analysis are more fully explained in the Appendix.

The UK Central Statistical Office quarterly series for ICCs' profit commences in 1962 and so our period of analysis commences with the start of the first business cycle after that date. Table 7.1 charts the behaviour of the rate of profit, and our measure of total real income in the ICC sector, from 1963 to 1985, and places the five complete cycles that occurred between those dates. Cycle V ends in 1981 quarter 1 and from that date to the present the UK private

Table 7 1   Rate of profit and real income in the UK ICC sector

Cycle	Phase	Quarter	$\bar{Y}$ £ million 1980 prices	Π/K per cent[1]
		1963(1)	16949.6	13.15
I	A			
		1964(2)	19373.4	17.66
I	B			
		1966(3)	20481.2	15.20
I	C			
		1967(3)	19713.2	13.52
II	A			
		1968(3)	21054.9[2]	15.92
II	B			
		1970(4)	20744.6	13.20
II	C			
		1972(1)	19677.5	12.56
III	A			
		1973(1)	22186.7	15.99
III	C			
		1974(1)	18921.7	7.04
IV	A			
		1974(2)	20243.8	9.80
IV	B			
		1975(1)	20503.7	7.46
IV	C			
		1976(2)	19604.4	5.95
V	A			
		1978(1)	21562.3	10.45
V	B			
		1978(3)	22136.1	10.31
V	C			
		1981(1)	18842.0	3.65
VI	A			
		1985(3)	23509.0	10.24

Source: see Appendix to chapter.

Notes to table:

1 Since a quarterly rate of profit series is a quarterly income flow divided by a stock measure the data presented are multiplied by four to give an annualized equivalent.

2 The data show that real income peaks in cycle II in 1968:3. However the time series plot suggests that this is something of a 'blip', and that after a decline in 1968:4 real output continues on an upward trend until 1970:4.

sector has been experiencing a steady and protracted boom. There is tentative evidence of a downturn in our profit series at 1985 quarter 3, though this may be very temporary and the result of the collapse in world crude oil prices. So, as for the USA, we provisionally date an additional cycle phase (phase VIA) from 1981 quarter 1 to 1985 quarter 3. As can be seen in all but one cycle (cycle III) there is evidence of a premature peak in the rate of profit, allowing us to distinguish Weisskopf's three-cycle phases for the UK. Cycle III coincides with the Conservative government's 'dash for growth' boom of 1972 to 1973 which was curtailed rather suddenly in the second half of 1973 by the first of the OPEC oil price increases. Hence real income during these two years shows a large fluctuation and the rate of profit and real income peak simultaneously in 1973 quarter 1.

A small number of previous studies have attempted to provide simple decompositions of the very basic components of the rate of profit for the UK manufacturing sector, using annual data. These results are problematic in that the use of annual data precludes the precise dating of the phases of each cycle. They therefore tend merely to calculate growth rates of the component variables from one year to the next. Hargreaves-Heap (1980) uses OECD data to provide a comparison of the profitability crisis in various OECD economies including the UK. He finds that a rising capital-output ratio is of particular importance in explaining the declining profit rate. For the UK Hargreaves-Heap points to the rise in the relative price of raw materials since 1973 and to real wages rising over the secular period faster than real productivity (what he terms 'the translation of labour purchased into labour performed').

Funke's (1986) results confirm the view that the behaviour of the profit rate at the beginning and the end of each cycle is matched by changes in profit share and the rate of capacity utilization. He also finds similar evidence to that of Weisskopf for a premature profit squeeze within each cycle before the output peak, and that this squeeze is matched by downward pressure on profit share. Particularly in the 1950s and 1960s it is the case that in the important phase B of each cycle the decline in profit rate coincides exclusively with a decline in profit share, suggesting a distributional shift explanation for the intra-cycle profit squeeze. In the 1970s the decline in the rate of capital productivity also contributes but is not of the same order of magnitude. For the secular period it seems that only in the mid-1970s is declining capacity utilization a significant contributory factor to the profit rate decline. Auerbach and Skott (1988) present annual data on gross profit share and the rate of capacity utilization and demonstrate the close secular correspondence between the two. Both show a downward trend between the 1961 to 1964 cycle to the 1974 to 1979 cycle. They argue that such evidence runs contrary to the predictions of rising monopolization theories, which would require rising profit share and falling utilization over the trend, and must therefore be explained by increasing competition, particularly foreign competition.

In Table 7.2 we present results for the simple decomposition contained in equation 5.7. The results for the intra-cycle breakdown confirm those of Funke (1986), showing a close correspondence between changes in profit rate and profit share. On average capacity utilization and capital productivity move with the profit rate, but their growth rates are much smaller. From cycle to cycle, however, it seems that changes in capital productivity become more important and certainly between cycles I and II and cycles II and III is generally the significant contributor to profit rate decline. Between cycles III and IV the sharp fall in profit rate coincides with a sharp fall in profit share and the very slight recovery in the profit rate between cycles IV and V is due to an improvement in profit share working against the continued decline in capital productivity. Capacity utilization has a small, but reinforcing, effect on profit rate decline, except between cycles II and III. These results are confirmed by the full period growth rates. The profit rate on average declines at just over 5 per cent per annum and approximately half of this decline comes from the decline in the profit share and nearly half from capital productivity, with a remaining small reinforcing effect from declining capacity utilization.

Table 7.2   Simple decomposition of changes in the rate of profit in the UK ICC sector

	Average annual exponential percentage rates of growth			
	$\dot{\Pi/K}$	$\dot{\sigma_\Pi}$	$\dot{U}$	$\dot{\theta}$
Phase averages[1]				
A	41.91	34.10	3.15	4.66
B	−10.84	−9.98	−0.66	−0.21
C	−31.44	−21.50	−2.19	−7.75
Between cycles[2]				
I–II	−3.77	−1.18	−0.31	−2.28
II–III	−3.19	−0.33	−0.06	−2.93
III–IV	−22.05	−16.61	−1.49	−3.96
IV–V	0.28	1.70	−0.38	−1.04
Full period[3]				
IA to VC	−5.89	−3.01	−0.42	−2.46
IB to VIA	−5.29	−2.74	−0.43	−2.11

Source: see Appendix to chapter.

1 The growth rate for each variable in each phase is computed as $100 \times (\log x(t_2) - \log x(t_1)) / (t_2 - t_1)$, where $x(t_1)$ and $x(t_2)$ refer to values at the start and end of a phase, and $t_2 - t_1$ is the length of phase in years. Phase averages are calculated as simple averages of these individual phase growth rates.

2 Computed as above but $x(t_1)$ and $x(t_2)$ are in this case geometric means of the variables for each cycle and are ascribed to the mid-point of the cycle, and $t_2 - t_1$ measures the time between these mid-points in years.

3 Obtained by estimating an ordinary least squares regression of $\log (x)$ on a constant and time (measured in years), and multiplying the slope coefficient from this regression by 100.

The figures in Table 7.2 give the actual behaviour of the different components of the rate of profit. In Table 7.3 we report results obtained once we have corrected for the under-utilization of non-production staff. As we would expect these show that declining capacity utilization is responsible over the secular period for a greater element of the profit rate decline than would appear from Table 7.2. It now appears that declining capacity productivity and declining profit share are of equal importance in explaining profit rate decline in the UK, although utilization conditions are now of greater quantitative importance. This result contrasts with the results for the USA where capital productivity provides virtually no explanation for profitability decline. The full period decline

Table 7.3   Decomposition of changes in the rate of profit with adjustment for under-utilization of labour in the UK ICC sector

	Average annual exponential percentage rates of growth			
	$\dot{\Pi/K}$	$\dot{\sigma}_\Pi^*$	$\dot{U}^*$	$\dot{\Theta}$
Phase averages				
A	41.91	30.48	6.78	4.66
B	−10.84	−9.01	−1.62	−0.21
C	−31.44	−18.40	−5.29	−7.75
Between cycles				
I–II	3.77	−0.82	−0.67	−2.28
II–III	−3.19	−12.36	12.10	−2.93
III–IV	−22.05	−14.54	−3.56	−3.96
IV–V	0.28	2.38	−1.06	−1.04
Full period				
IA to VC	−5.89	−2.38	−1.05	−2.46
IB to VIA	−5.29	−1.98	−1.20	−2.11

Source: see Appendix to chapter.
Notes: see Table 7.2.

in adjusted capacity utilization between 1962 and 1982 of 1 per cent per annum compares with a full period decline of 0.6 per cent per annum for the USA for the period 1949–1982. So in absolute terms it appears that declining utilization may be of slightly greater importance in the UK than in the USA. Since the profit rate decline in the UK is much faster than in the USA the contribution of the other two factors of adjusted profit share and capital productivity are in absolute terms considerably greater than for the USA.

Turning to the between-cycle analysis we see that from cycle I to cycle II the declining capital productivity explanation is quantitatively of greatest importance. Distributional shift and capacity utilization contribute to profit rate decline but at rates of less than 1 percentage point per annum. In the cycle II to III period the results show the very pronounced effect of the Heath–Barber boom of 1972 to 1973, in the very sharp improvement in capacity utilization. Nevertheless the effect of this increase in utilization is completely wiped out by the adverse distribution shift. Again between these cycles we observe the steady decline in capital productivity, and this decline continues between cycles III and IV. The sharp adverse distributional shift continues between cycles III and IV, and is now reinforced by an appreciable fall (3.56 per cent per annum) in capacity utilization conditions. Finally between cycles IV and V the downward trend in the profit rate is reversed. This appears to be due to two factors. First, the rates of decline of capital productivity and capacity utilization slow down and second, the distribution shift during this period is in favour of profit share.

Looking at the intra-cycle phase average results and making comparison with Table 7.2 we see that in the important phase B the adverse distributional shift (contributing *ceteris paribus* 9 percentage points to the fall in the rate of profit) is still the important feature. The decline in utilization conditions is now more pronounced (contributing *ceteris paribus* 1.6 percentage points to the profit rate fall) showing that as each expansion progresses output growth fails to match firms' expansion of productive capacity.

Table 7.4 shows the further of breakdown of adjusted profit share and capital productivity given by equations 5.11 and 5.12. For the adjusted profit share breakdown the growth rate of each

Table 7.4 Breakdown of changes in capital productivity and adjusted profit share in the UK ICC sector

	Average annual exponential percentage rates of growth				
	1	2	3	4	5
Adjusted profit share	$\dot{\sigma}_\Pi^{*}$	$-\Phi\dot{\bar{\sigma}}_w^{*}$	$-\Phi\dot{\bar{w}}^{*}$	$\Phi\dot{\bar{y}}^{*}$	$-\Phi(\dot{P}_w-\dot{P}_y)$
Phase averages					
A	30.48	33.67	−17.74	51.41	−3.19
B	−9.01	−16.29	−29.56	13.29	7.28
C	−18.40	−18.09	3.94	22.03	−0.31
Between cycles					
I–II	−0.82	0.34	−10.40	10.74	−1.16
II–III	−12.36	−4.15	−9.76	5.61	−8.21
III–IV	−14.53	−18.08	−13.57	−4.51	3.54
IV–V	2.38	4.01	−4.38	8.39	−1.63
Full period					
IA to VC	−2.38	−3.37	−11.05	7.68	0.99
IB to VIA	−1.98	−2.53	−9.96	7.43	0.55

	1	2	3	4
Capital productivity	$\dot{\theta}$	$\dot{\bar{y}}^{*}$	$\dot{\bar{j}}^{*}$	$\dot{P}_y-\dot{P}_k$
Phase averages				
A	4.66	11.82	5.33	−1.84
B	−0.21	3.02	5.23	2.01
C	−7.75	−4.87	2.31	−0.57
Between cycles				
I–II	−2.28	3.25	6.11	0.58
II–III	−2.93	1.61	2.84	−1.69
III–IV	−3.96	−1.04	2.16	−0.76
IV–V	−1.04	1.98	2.74	−0.28

	Average annual exponential percentage rates of growth			
	1	2	3	4
Full period				
IA to VC	−2.46	1.75	3.78	−0.43
IB to VIA	−2.11	1.63	3.42	−0.32

Source: see Appendix to chapter.
Notes: see Table 7.2.

component of truly required wage share is multiplied by the multiplier, Φ, in order that the figures shown give the percentage point contribution of the change in each component to change in profit rate. The full period results show the persistent decline in capital productivity comes about through a failure of the growth of truly required real labour productivity to keep pace with the growth of the truly required real capital–labour ratio. This depressant effect is reinforced by a small adverse price effect brought about by capital goods prices rising faster than output price. The adverse secular movement in the truly required profit share can be seen to be accounted for by the growth in the truly required real labour share – because the real wage[3] grows faster than real productivity. Price movements counteract this effect to a limited extent since the price of wage goods tends not to rise as fast as output price.

Table 7.4 shows that the same explanation holds here for the between-cycle periods as for the full period – growth of labour productivity failing to keep pace with the capital–labour ratio. In the final cycle-to-cycle period truly required profit share recovers (as does actual profit share). This is accounted for by a recovery in productivity sufficient to generate, *ceteris paribus*, an 8.4 per cent improvement in the rate of profit. Real wage growth during this period does not wholly cancel out this productivity improvement. From the intra-cycle analysis in Table 7.4 we see that the important distributional shift in phase B is entirely accounted for by a rise in the truly required real labour share, generated by real wage growth outstripping productivity growth. Price changes in fact serve to mitigate this effect.

Overall these results would seem to point to an explanation for profit rate decline accounted for by labour productivity growth that has failed to keep pace with, first, the growth in the real wage, and second, the growth in the capital–labour ratio. This has generated a rising labour share and a declining level of capital productivity respectively. Over the secular period it seems that these real effects are dominant and that price movements contribute little to the profit squeeze. These effects have been combined with a secular tendency, until 1981, for the level of capacity utilization to decline.

ACCOUNTING FOR THE COMPOSITION OF AGGREGATE LABOUR SHARE IN THE UK

In this section we present results for the breakdown of 'labour income' into the three components of production workers' wages, non-production staff salaries and, in the UK case, employers' labour tax (equation 4.16). Figure 7.1 plots the behaviour of these three since 1962. Using UK data we are only able to include employers' national insurance contributions in the third component. Since these are not accumulated on an actuarial basis but rather included by the UK government in its overall taxation receipts then they can be regarded as a form of labour tax. No data are available to account for private provision of health and pension insurance and other forms of private deferred payment. In any case private insurance provision has, until recently, been of much lesser importance in the UK than in the USA. Table 7.5 gives phase average, between-cycle and full period growth rates for both the actual levels of total labour share and its three components, and for their real truly required levels after adjustment for utilization of overhead labour. So for example we see that looking at the full period from the start of cycle I to the end of cycle V (IA–VC) then actual total labour share rises by 0.69 per cent per annum. On the other hand because over this period capacity utilization declines, and wage goods prices rise faster than output prices then the real truly required share rises by 0.77 per cent per annum. However if we measure the full period growth rate from the start of phase IB to the end of phase VIA then the real true growth rate

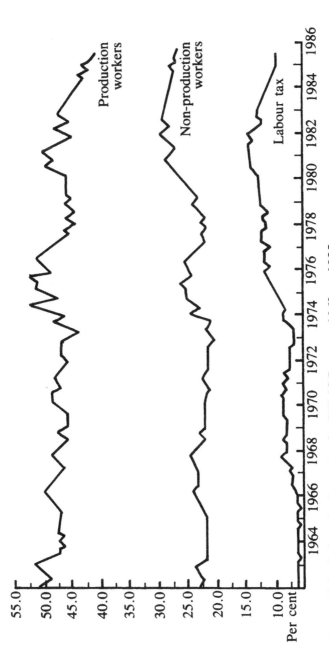

Figure 7.1 Labour's shares in the UK ICC sector 1962 to 1985

Table 7.5 Composition of labour share in the UK ICC sector

Changes in unadjusted	Average annual exponential percentage rates of growth			
components	1	2	3	4
	σ_w	W_d/Y	W_o/Y	C/Y
Phase averages				
A	−7.84	−8.43	−6.06	−4.21
B	2.27	1.75	2.84	3.97
C	4.75	3.29	6.04	9.09
Between cycles				
I–II	0.36	−0.47	0.62	5.20
II–III	0.00	0.25	−0.48	−0.07
III–IV	3.84	2.72	3.87	9.87
IV–V	−0.40	−2.02	−0.06	6.00
Full period				
IA to VC	0.69	−0.33	1.20	4.73
IB to VIA	0.60	−0.09	0.74	3.71
Changes in truly required				
shares	1	2	3	4
	$\sigma_w^{*\prime}$	$\overline{W}_d/\overline{Y}$	$\overline{W}_o^{*}/\overline{Y}$	$\overline{C}^{*}/\overline{Y}$
Phase averages				
A	−7.63	−9.18	−5.51	−3.99
B	3.72	3.41	3.85	5.42
C	3.94	3.22	3.77	8.29
Between cycles				
I–II	−0.10	−0.83	−0.05	4.74
II–III	1.00	1.21	0.55	0.93
III–IV	4.18	3.53	3.20	10.21
IV–V	−0.95	−2.40	−0.82	5.46

	Average annual exponential percentage rates of growth			
Changes in truly required shares	1	2	3	4
Full period	$\sigma_W^{*\prime}$	$\overline{W}_d/\overline{Y}$	$\overline{W}_o^{*}/\overline{Y}$	$\overline{C}^{*}/\overline{Y}$
IA to VC	0.77	0.14	0.55	4.81
IB to VIA	0.56	−0.21	0.88	3.66

Source: see Appendix to chapter.
Notes: see Table 7.2.

is lower than the actual growth rate. This is because in phase 6A capacity utilization improves.

The breakdown of the full period results show that for actual shares production worker share falls very slightly over the full period, whereas overhead staff share rises and the share of employers' labour tax rises significantly. On the other hand a fall in the truly required real production worker share is only detected for the IB to VIA full period. This result contrasts with that for the USA in Chapter 6 where real truly required production worker share displays a pronounced downward trend of 1 per cent per annum for the full period and downwards for each between-cycle period, moving quite clearly in the opposite direction to the other components. The between-cycle direction of growth for truly required real non-production and real production shares matches that for the total share. So we find little evidence for the UK, in contrast to the USA, of a secular distributional drift away from production staff towards non-production staff. On the other hand the growth of non-wage costs as a share of income is as pronounced in the UK as it was found to be for the USA.

Furthermore the intra-cycle results shown here for the UK contrast with those for the USA. The results for the UK, for both actual and real truly required shares, show that total labour share and its three components all fall in phase B, increase again in phase B and continue to increase in phase C. So it appears that all the components of labour income contribute to the downward pressure on the rate of profit in phase B. These averages hide the experience of individual cycles, but the only principal exception to this average pattern is in cycle V, 1976 quarter 2 to 1981 quarter 1, when in phase B both real production worker share and the real truly required share of labour tax fall. The overall slight increase in the total share in the phase comes about because the share of non-production staff rises.

For the USA it was found that only the share of production workers behaves according to this anticyclical pattern with a premature upturn in phase B. Non-production staff share moves over the cycle following the same pattern as profit share, procyclically with a premature downturn in phase B, and the share of non-wage costs on average across all cycles increases in each phase.

All this suggests that there is very slight evidence of a distributional shift away from production staff over the secular time period, but no evidence of the significant decline observed for the USA. Furthermore there is no evidence for the UK of a procyclical non-production staff 'managerial' share that mirrors the behaviour of profit share. The principal similarity between UK and USA is to be found in the secular growth in non-wage labour costs. UK statistics do not allow for analysis of non-statutory non-wage costs, as is possible in the USA. However it seems likely that if these were separated from wage and salary payments then the growth in non-wage costs would be accentuated. As it is we have found that the secular growth in total labour income comes about as a result of a growing 'tax wedge'.

WAGE SHARE AND THE DEGREE OF MONOPOLY IN UK MANUFACTURING

Table 7.6 shows the behaviour of the three components of the Kaleckian wage share identity, equation 2.7, for the UK manufacturing sector since 1948, consistent with the data shown for the USA in Table 5.6. It shows clearly the steady sustained downward movement in production worker wage share of value added. The movement in the revenue–cost margin (k) is plotted in Figure 7.2. The upward trend in the series since the end of the Second World War is quite pronounced, and although the series shows a sharp temporary drop in 1974, the upward trend continues through the 1970s and 1980s. This sustained upward trend contrasts

Table 7.6 UK manufacturing: production wage share, the aggregate revenue-cost margin and ratio of wages to materials 1948-1986

Averages	Production worker wage share of value added (per cent)	Revenue– cost margin[1] (per cent)	Ratio of materials bill to production wage bill
1948	42.4	21.4	3.337
1949–51	42.5	19.7	3.948
1954	41.3	21.0	3.758
1955–57	42.9	21.2	3.708
1958	41.0	21.0	4.017
1963	36.8	24.6	3.715
1968	34.5	25.9	3.896
1970–72	34.4	26.8	3.809
1973–75	33.1	27.1	4.297
1976–78	31.5	26.8	4.785
1979–81	31.0	28.9	4.265
1982–84	27.8	30.6	4.685
1985–86	26.5	31.2	4.858

Sources:
1947–1970: *Historical Record of the Census of Production 1907–1970*, HMSO, 1979; *1971–1986 Census of Production*, Summary Tables, HMSO (various years).

1 Computed as (value added minus operatives wages)/gross output.

with the USA where the same series reaches a plateau in 1970. However the same caveats should be made in interpreting movements in this series, as where pointed out for the USA. Upward movement need not imply upward movement in the 'degree of monopoly'. First, any secular movement towards higher levels of vertical integration would impart an upward movement to the series. Second, any downward movement in the level of capacity utilization would increase the burden of fixed costs and produce an upward movement in the series. In the 1970s faltering

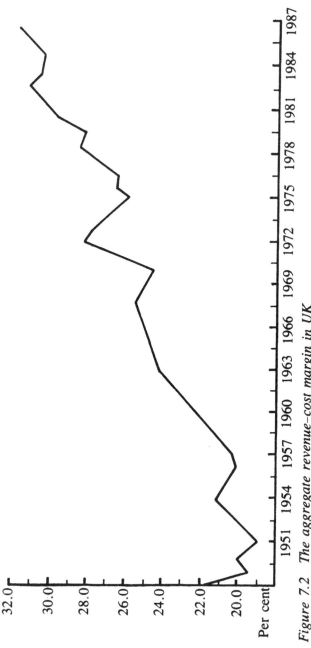

Figure 7.2 The aggregate revenue–cost margin in UK manufacturing industry 1948–1986

levels of aggregate demand may well have led to this taking place. A comparison of the growth rates of actual and truly required non-production worker share in Table 7.5 does show from cycle III onwards that the between-cycle growth rates of truly required salary share are not as high as the actual growth rates. Between cycles VI and V, covering the late 1970s and early 1980s, the actual share falls by only 0.06 per cent per annum but the truly required share falls by 0.82 per cent per annum. The decline in capacity utilization in manufacturing in the mid-1970s and early 1980s was rather more pronounced than for the rest of the corporate sector of the UK economy, and so it may be that the rise in the revenue–cost margin in the manufacturing sector in the 1970s and 1980s is explained by this decline. Table 7.6 also shows for the 1970s the impact on the ratio of materials costs to wages costs of sharply rising energy costs in the 1970s. The impact of these seems to have been felt on wage share rather than on price–cost margins.

In contrast the 1960s were a period of sustained high levels of capacity utilization and stable raw materials costs. As for the USA it seems likely that if a rising concentration explanation for the upward movement in the revenue–cost margin is to be sustained then it is most plausible during this period. Evidence on movements in both aggregate concentration and in industrial concentration tend to support this. Prais (1976) presents evidence on the sharp upward movement in aggregate concentration in British manufacturing industry from 1949 to 1970. The 100 firm concentration ratio rises from 22 per cent to 41 per cent between those two dates. This growth is considerably steeper than observed for the USA and is attributed by most authors in particular to the merger wave of the 1960s (Hannah 1983, Curry and George 1983). Hughes and Kumar (1984a, 1984b) report evidence on aggregate concentration for the whole British corporate sector from 1972 until 1982, and find that aggregate concentration continues to increase sharply until 1976. They report for the whole UK quoted company sector a rise between 1972 and 1976 of 10 percentage points in the 100-firm concentration ratio. This general trend is robust to a variety of different methods of measurement of concentration. In the late 1970s aggregate concentration falls but not sufficiently to offset the upward movement observed for the first half of the decade. A number of studies find that average industrial concentration in

British manufacturing rose during the 1950s and 1960s, although there appears to have been little change since the late 1960s (Curry and George 1983). Merger activity was intense once again in the mid-1980s; however evidence on changes in aggregate and industrial concentration tends to be reported with a long publication lag and so it is not yet possible to assess whether this has had any impact on concentration levels. So as for the USA we must conclude that any suggestion of a Kaleckian degree of monopoly explanation for movements in wage share is most likely to be sustained for the 1960s.

THE PROFIT REVIVAL OF THE 1980s

In this concluding section of the chapter we investigate the revival in profits that appears to have occurred since 1981. This revival is most pronounced in the aggregate real gross trading profits data, which show that real profits for the ICC sector when deflated by the GDP deflator have risen from under £6 billion (at 1980 prices) in 1981 to a temporary peak in 1985 quarter 3 of £10.5 billion, and by 1987 to well above £11 billion. The net profit rate data show a less pronounced, but nevertheless significant rise (see Table 7.1). As explained earlier we have tentatively dated the end of the first phase of the cycle in corporate real output at 1985 quarter 3 (phase VIA), and in Table 7.7 we present the average annual percentage growth rates of the components of both the profit rate decomposition and the decomposition of labour share.

The results in Table 7.7 suggest that phase VIA shows the typical characteristics of other cycle phase As. The 22.9 per cent annual increase in the rate of profit seems large, but a comparison with Table 7.3 shows that this rate of increase is well below the average for a phase A. Typically for a phase A most of this profit rate growth comprises growth in profit share – profit share adjusted for utilization conditions contributes over 16 percentage points of this growth per annum. The remaining 6.5 points arise from a 4 per cent growth from capacity utilization and a 2.5 per cent growth in capital productivity. Again a comparison with Table 7.3 shows these growth rates are below average. The decomposition of adjusted profit share shows that the distribution shift in favour of

Table 7.7 Annual rates of growth of components of rate of profit during phase 6A 1981(q1) to 1985(q3) in the UK ICC sector

		%
Rate of profit	$\dot{\Pi}/K$	22.92
Profit share	$\dot{\sigma}_{\Pi}$	19.28
Adjusted profit share	$\dot{\sigma}_{\Pi}^{*}$	16.27
Contribution of		
– real truly req. labour share	$-\dot{\Phi}\bar{\sigma}_{w}$	21.06
– real truly req. wage	$-\dot{\Phi}\bar{w}^{*}$	−16.39
– real truly req. lab. productivity	$-\dot{\Phi}\bar{y}^{*}$	37.45
– relative prices	$-\Phi(\dot{P}_{w}-\dot{P}_{Y})$	−4.79
Capacity utilization	$\dot{U}$	1.13
Adjusted capacity utilization	$\dot{U}^{*}$	4.14
Capital productivity	$\dot{\theta}$	2.51
– real truly req. lab. productivity	$\bar{y}^{*}$	6.51
– real truly req. capital–lab. ratio	$\dot{j}$	4.99
– relative prices	$\dot{P}_{y}-\dot{P}_{k}$	0.99
Labour share decomposition		
real truly req. total labour share	$\bar{\sigma}_{w}^{*\,\prime}$	−3.83
– real production labour share	$\overline{W}_{d}/\overline{Y}$	−4.38
– real truly req. non-production labour share	$\overline{W}_{o}^{*}/\overline{Y}$	−1.04
– real truly req. employers labour tax share	$\overline{C}^{*}/\overline{Y}$	−7.83

Source: see Appendix to chapter.

profit is entirely explained by the 37.45 percentage point contribution to profit rate growth from labour productivity growth. This considerably exceeds the (negative) contribution generated by real wage growth. However large as this productivity contribution may seem it is also below the phase average, and indeed phase A is typically a period in which productivity growth well exceeds real wage growth. Therefore the only novel feature of phase VIA that has caused current levels of profitability to be high is its length – no other phase A since 1962 (or probably before that) has enjoyed four and a half years of sustained productivity growth without real wage pressure placing upward pressure on real wage share.

Examination of the decomposition of real truly required labour share suggests shows that most of the reduction in the share arises from falls in the share of production workers and in the share of the employers' labour tax burden. The fall in this latter share is well above the phase A average (see Table 7.5). Non-production staff appear to have lost ground least in the distributional shift away from labour income to profit income.

CONCLUSIONS

The decomposition of the rate of profit for the UK corporate sector between 1963 and the present has revealed a number of interesting conclusions about profit rate behaviour. Over the full period from 1963 to 1985 the net profit rate declined on average by over 5 per cent per annum. This compares with a decline of only 1 per cent per annum for the USA for the period 1949 to 1982. It appears that all three of our major components of profit rate, namely capital productivity, capacity utilization conditions and distribution conditions, contribute significantly to this decline. The capacity utilization contribution is the least important of the three. The decomposition of the decline in capital productivity and in profit share (adjusted for utilization conditions) shows that in both cases the decline appears to be explained by inadequate labour productivity growth. In the case of capital productivity labour productivity growth fails to match growth in the capital–labour ratio, and in the case of profit share (or conversely wage share) labour productivity growth fails to match real labour earnings growth. The latter argument is consistent with the Kilpatrick and Lawson (1980) explanation for British industrial decline. We can draw out two important differences here with the American experience. First, both Weisskopf's results for the period 1949 to 1975 and the present authors' for the 1949 to 1985 period show that changes in capital productivity are unimportant in explaining profit rate decline in the USA. Second, in the UK the secular decline in profit share (rise in labour share) is the result of real factors (real wage growth exceeding real productivity growth) whereas in the USA it is the consequence of adverse price movements (the price of wage goods not rising as fast as the price of output). As mentioned in Chapter 5 Weisskopf (1979) terms the distinction between these two effects as one of 'offensive' and 'defensive' labour strength.

Within each business we observe a similar pattern to the USA, with a premature peak in the rate of profit coinciding with upward pressure on real wage share. This phenomenon of rising real wage share can be conversely seen as one of a falling real profit margin, and so over the secular period is entirely consistent with either a 'labour power' hypothesis or the rising international competition hypothesis often mooted for the UK (Glyn and Sutcliffe 1972). However Funke (1986) rejects this latter hypothesis on the basis of his evidence for the UK manufacturing sector.

The results presented here for the breakdown in labour share suggest that a rising labour power hypothesis for the secular period is too simplistic, although within cycles we find evidence that all the components of labour share start to rise in the important phase B. The results suggest for the secular period that rising labour share can be largely accounted for by the rising share of employers' national insurance contributions up to 1979, and the inability of firms to pass this rising burden of taxation on into higher product prices. As for the USA evidence shows a slight overall decline in actual wage share since the 1960s. For the manufacturing sector alone this decline is considerably more pronounced. However if this movement is to be explained by movements in corporate market power then it seems that evidence for this is only strong for the 1960s.

Finally our methodology has enabled us to cast some light on the post-1980 profitability revival that has been experienced by the UK corporate sector. It appears that there is no evidence to support a notion of a 'breakthrough' in terms of higher growth rates of any of the components, particularly labour productivity. The restoration of the rate of profit to a figure approaching pre-1974 levels (and probably beyond since 1985) has arisen as a result of the length of the sustained upswing in the early and mid-1980s, which has been maintained without the onset of the usual mid-cycle distributional pressure. The slight decline in our measure of rate of profit in 1985 and 1986 is probably the result of the impact of falling oil prices on the North Sea Oil sector, and in fact as far as the rest of the corporate sector is concerned, profit rates still reflect the experience of the initial upswing period of a very long business cycle.

APPENDIX

Data sources and definitions

All data series are seasonably adjusted quarterly series unless otherwise indicated.

Π Net pre-tax profit of ICCs, current prices.
        This was derived as $P + R - CC$. P is the gross trading profits of ICCs including profits of North Sea Oil companies, net of stock appreciation, current prices (*source* ETAS). R is rent and non-trading income of ICCs, current prices (*source* ETAS). CC is capital consumption of ICCs and was linearly interpolated from annual data (*source* UKNA, table 13.3).

K Net capital stock, current prices.
        The starting point for this series was annual data for net capital stock in the ICC sector at current replacement cost (*source* UKNA, table 13.7). This annual series was converted into a quarterly series using quarterly data on ICC net investment. A quarterly net investment series was obtained by subtracting linearly interpolated capital consumption (see above) from gross domestic fixed capital formation of ICCs (*source* ETAS).

U Capacity utilization.
        This is derived as the ratio of actual GDP to potential GDP. Actual GDP is GDP at factor cost in current prices (*source*

ETAS). Potential GDP was obtained from Layard and Nickell (1986b, pp. s368-s374). The Layard and Nickell series is annual, and quarterly data was interpolated from this. Interpolation in this case should result in no loss of information for a potential output series should exhibit no seasonal variation. One further problem arises with the Layard and Nickell series in that it ends in 1983. 1984 and 1985 data points were obtained on the basis of extrapolation using a quartic time trend fitted to the period 1953 to 1983. The resulting series was then keyed from 1975 to 1980 prices, using the actual GDP deflator. The Layard and Nickell series is computed, using a Cobb–Douglas production function approach which includes adjustment for labour-augmenting technical progress, as follows:

$$\Delta \log Y^p = (1-v)\Delta \log L + v\Delta \log K + (1+v)\Delta \log A$$

where Y^p is potential GDP, L the labour force, K gross total capital stock, v is a measure of profit share of national income. Δ indicates the annual change. A an index of labour-augmented technical progress is computed as follows:

$$\Delta \log A = \frac{1}{(1-v)} (\Delta \log Y^a - (1-v)\Delta \log N - v\Delta \log K)$$

where Y^a is actual GDP at factor cost, and N is employment. The sources of Y^a, L, N, K and v are detailed in Layard and Nickell (1986b). Y^p was, in initial analysis, obtained directly from the preceding equations using quarterly (though for some series interpolated) data for the variables given in CLEDB, rather than by interpolation from Layard and Nickell's published annual series. However the resulting series displayed an increase in the rate of growth of potential GDP from 1982, in contrast to the series constructed as above which displays a slowing down of the rate of increase in potential GDP from about 1980. This increase is generated by the behaviour of the index of technical progress which has a probable upward bias imparted by the dramatic collapse in employment from 1981. The interpolated series seemed considerably more plausible, being consistent with the evidence on premature scrapping and decline in the manufacturing sector capital stock presented by Wadhwani and Wall (1986), and so was used in obtaining the reported results.

W Total income from employment in the ICC sector, current prices.

Annual data on income from employment in the ICC sector in current prices, W_a (*source* UKNA, table 2.5), were interpolated to obtain a quarterly series, using quarterly data on total income from employment for the whole economy in current prices, TW_t. It was assumed that seasonal variation in the (unknown) ICC series matched that for the whole economy, so between year-end quarterly figures were computed as follows:

$$W_{t+i} = (W_a/4) \cdot (TW_t/TW_{t+i}) \qquad i = 0,1,2,3$$

Y Total net income ICC sector, current prices.
This is simply the sum of Π and W. Therefore labour share, σ_W, and profit share, σ_Π, sum to unity.

Z Capacity net income ICC sector, current prices.
This is computed by dividing total net income by the capacity utilization rate.

$\hat{U}$ Optimal capacity utilization rate.
Weisskopf (1979) sets this arbitrarily at 0.9. However he uses the published Federal Reserve estimates of US manufacturing capacity utilization which rarely exceeds 90 per cent. Our series for the UK on a couple of occasions exceeds 97 per cent, and so we set the optimal rate at 1.0. In fact this value is unimportant since it only affects the levels of the key variables and does not affect rates of growth, which form the basis of the reported results.

w_dL_d Production staff wage bill (wage · employment).

w_oL_o Non-production staff wage bill.

It is not possible to obtain a direct breakdown of the wage bill for the ICC sector into production and non-production staff, so W was divided between production and non-production staff using data linearly interpolated from a published annual series for manufacturing industry giving the ratio of production worker wages to administrative, technical and clerical salaries (*source* UKNA 1959–1969, Census of Production 1970 to 1985).

L Total employment in the non-financial private sector.

This was estimated as total employees in employment (source AAS) less employees in employment in the insurance, banking and finance sector (source AAS) and in the public sector (source 1962–1975 HLS, 1976–85 OECD). The sources detailed provided annual mid-year estimates and a quarterly series was obtained as for W using the quarterly index of employment in manufacturing industries, 1980=100 (source ETAS).

L_d Production staff employment.

L_o Non-production staff employment.

As with the wage bill it is not possible to obtain a direct breakdown for the ICC sector so as before employment was allocated between the two groups using linearly interpolated data from annual data for the percentage of administrative, technical and clerical staff in manufacturing industry (*source* AAS).

P_y Output price deflator, 1980=1.

This was approximated by the GDP deflator, the ratio of GDP at factor cost in current prices to GDP at factor cost in 1980 prices (*source* ETAS).

P_w Wage goods price deflator, 1980=1.
This was approximated by the retail price index for all
items, 1975=100 (*source* ETAS), which was seasonally
adjusted using a moving arithmetic average and keyed to
1980=1.

P_k Capital good price index, 1980=1.
This was computed as the implicit deflator for private sector
gross domestic fixed capital formation; the ratio of private
sector gross domestic fixed capital formation in current
prices to the same in 1980 prices (*source* ETAS). Consistent
current and constant price series were only available in
unadjusted form and so the ratio was seasonally adjusted
using a moving arithmetic average.

j^* Real truly required capital–labour ratio.
Computed as real capital stock divided by truly required
employment, L^*.

C Employers' labour tax bill.
This is calculated as $C = t\, W$, where t is the employers'
tax rate. $(1 + t)$ is calculated as the ratio of an index of
labour costs per unit of output, 1980=100 to an index of
wages and salaries per unit of output, 1980=100. Both
series were obtained in unadjusted, quarterly form from
CLEDB, and seasonally adjusted using a moving arithmetic
average. This provides an index of $(1 + t)$ based at 1980.
The series was scaled by taking the effective employers'
National Insurance rate implied by the ratio of national
insurance costs to total labour costs for manufacturing
industry for 1980, obtained from the 1980 Census of
Production. t for 1980 turns out to be 0.178.

C_d, C_o Employers' labour tax bill for production and non-
production staff.
Since national insurance contributions are paid as a constant
percentage of earnings then it is appropriate to allocate C
between the two types of labour according to the proportion

of production and non-production staff in the total wage bill. So:

$$C_d = W_d / (W_d + W_o) \cdot C \text{ and}$$
$$C_o = W_o / (W_d + W_o) \cdot C$$

Abbreviations

AAS   *Annual Abstract of Statistics,* Central Statistical Office

CLEDB   Centre for Labour Economics, London School of Economics, quarterly database (Haskel 1987)

ETAS   *Economic Trends Annual Supplement,* Central Statistical Office

HLS   *Handbook of Labour Statistics,* Department of Employment, various annual issues up to 1976

OECD   *OECD National Accounts,* various years

UKNA   *United Kingdom National Accounts* (the Blue Book), Central Statistical Office (table nos refer to 1988 edition)

NOTES

1. This chapter incorporates and extends empirical work previously published as Henley (1989).
2. The profits from North Sea Oil operations are included. This is because, notwithstanding other arguments for and against the inclusion of income from North Sea Oil in a measure of UK private sector corporate income, it is not possible to obtain the other data used in the analysis for a definition of the ICC sector that excludes North Sea Oil.
3. The term 'wage' indicates average quarterly earnings of all employees, both production and non-production.

8. Distribution and the Political and Social Environment[1]

INTRODUCTION: KALECKI ON THE POLITICS OF FULL EMPLOYMENT

The purpose of this chapter is to widen our field of vision to discuss the links from the wider socio-economic and political environment to the distribution of income between labour income and profits. Chapters 6 and 7 have shown that the American and British economies exhibit considerable variation in income shares over the business cycle. The 'profit-squeeze' theories of cyclical movements in distribution suggest that the progress of each business cycle may see considerable variation in the relative bargaining strengths of employers and employed. So we discuss here the way in which distributional movements may both initiate and be initiated by changes in the socio-political balance between the two groups. One of the earliest and yet most influential attempts to deal with this is to be found in Kalecki's classic article 'Political Aspects of Full Employment', published in *The Political Quarterly* in 1943.[2] As a vehicle for this discussion the chapter begins by offering a reappraisal of Kalecki's ideas. These in essence revolve around issues of distributional conflict between wages and profits. Anyone re-reading Kalecki's paper with the benefit of 45 years' hindsight will be impressed by its contemporary relevance. For example, Malcolm Sawyer, already cited as a prominent authority on the economics of Kalecki, writes:

The experience of reading Kalecki some forty years after it was written makes one realise how ideas once thought dead come back to life. Allowing for some changes in the use of language, one finds Kalecki seeking to deal with a range of arguments used to justify unemployment and deflationary government policies which have again been at the forefront in the past decade. (Sawyer 1985, pp. 141-142)

In the intervening period between the publication of Kalecki's paper and the present day considerable resources of paper and ink have been allocated to discussion and elaboration of the relationship between political behaviour and macroeconomic policy making and performance. An aim of this chapter is therefore to suggest, in the light of 45 years of subsequent economic history, that within Kalecki's work are the germs of ideas about the long-run inter-relationship between economic policy, income distribution, and political and social change. Finally we shall look forward and attempt to suggest that Kalecki's ideas concerning these relationships may help to provide pointers to likely future economic performance in the British and American economies. We shall speculate about possible obstacles to further reductions in the level of unemployment, particularly in the British context where recent reductions in unemployment have only been at a slow rate.

Kalecki's original intention was to investigate the implications of what he thought to be the reluctance of capitalists to accept prolonged attempts by governments to use government expenditure to create and preserve conditions of full employment.[3] He was writing in the historical context of an emerging Keynesian policy consensus on both sides of the Atlantic, as exemplified by the Beveridge plan in the UK and the Full Employment Bill in the USA (enacted in 1949), for the reconstruction of peacetime economies under conditions of full employment. Elsewhere Kalecki had elaborated what he believed at the time to be the economic difficulties associated with policies aimed at preserving full employment. The discussion in Chapter 2 has touched on these. In his 1943 paper he attempts to identify specifically the political constraints facing such government action. In essence Kalecki argued that prolonged attempts at the maintenance of full employment might prove difficult for reasons associated with the dynamic behaviour of the capitalist economy and politically infeasible due to the political power of those controlling business and rentier interests. With the maturation of the capitalist economy declining levels of capacity utilization would in turn reduce the attractiveness of further investment, leading to a decline in aggregate demand and economic stagnation. Higher and higher levels of government deficit spending, or greater and greater efforts to stimulate private investment, would be required to circumvent such stagnationary forces.[4]

The political infeasibility of prolonged full employment maintenance would arise because capitalists would start to dislike the social and political consequences of such a state of affairs and would therefore bring pressure to bear on policy makers to initiate a change of direction. Specifically Kalecki identifies three reasons why capitalists would object. The first is a dislike of 'Government interference in the problem of unemployment as such'. This stems from the assertion that capitalists would desire a maintenance of the link between their own investment decisions and the state of the economy. Government interference in the *laissez-faire* system breaks that link and indeed growing government expenditures may undermine business confidence since capitalists would believe that future business prospects depend on the pursuit of 'sound' financial policies. Kalecki presumably felt that capitalists would remain sceptical about the efficacy of Keynesian-type policies. The second is a dislike of 'the direction of government spending'. In the broadest sense this stems from a fear on the part of capitalists of 'crowding out' under high levels of aggregate demand. Particularly in the medium and long-term government investment activity may become redirected away from social infrastructure to activities that are in direct competition with private sector business activities – so crowding out private investment in those activities. This may, Kalecki argues, result in attempts at the nationalization of traditionally private sector activities to provide continued outlets for government capital expenditure. On the consumption expenditure side Kalecki argues that capitalists would dislike the subsidization of mass consumption through government transfer payments and through price controls and subsidies on necessities (which might become necessary to control inflationary pressure in an economy running close to or at full employment). Specifically the subsidization of mass consumption contravenes the capitalist ethic that, as Kalecki vividly puts it, 'you shall earn your bread in sweat'. Third, and perhaps most importantly for the present discussion, they would begin to dislike the 'social and political changes resulting from the *maintenance* [Kalecki's own emphasis] of full employment' (Kalecki 1943, p. 326). These changes involve the diminution of the effectiveness of 'the sack' in maintaining labour discipline and hence a growth in the political power and consciousness of the working class with an accompanying undermining of the social position of the employing class. This is of course a very similar argument to that underlying the Marxist concept of the role of the reverse army. The strictly economic idea that falling unemployment increases upward pressure on real wages underpins the orthodox Phillips curve relationship (Phillips 1958). Kalecki's point provides a possible socio-political underpinning to the cyclical behaviour of profitability and output observed for the British and American economies in Chapters 6 and 7. The premature cyclical peak in profitability might be seen as indicative of the kind of political changes in the balance of power between capitalists and organized labour as each cyclical expansion progresses. Boddy and Crotty (1975) in particular place this interpretation on the cyclical behaviour of income shares.

THE POLITICAL BUSINESS CYCLE

The arguments outlined in the previous section led Kalecki to the prediction that capitalists' attitude to reflationary public expenditure would be ambivalent. Initial enthusiasm for, and encouragement of policies aimed at rejuvenating capitalists' markets through a tackling of the deficient level of aggregate demand in a depressed economy would eventually give way to scepticism concerning the efficacy of such an approach and lobbying for a change in policy direction. Accepting that the capitalist lobby is influential in the determination of government policy (and we shall examine this assumption more closely shortly) then it is clear that this tension between the economic advantages (employment creation) and the social, political and ideological disadvantages (as detailed above) of reflationary policy is likely to result in what Kalecki termed a 'political business cycle'. As the economy approaches full employment the political, social and ideological disadvantages start to outweigh the economic advantages. Labour discipline starts to break down and employers become anxious to 'teach them a lesson' (Kalecki 1943, p.329). In addition accelerating inflation would reduce the real value of debts, so devaluing the assets of the financial sector and leading to discontent among 'rentier' groups.

After a period of slump conditions political pressure would once more be voiced by capitalist/rentier groups for the government to do something to stimulate investment and aggregate demand. Hence it seems that Kalecki was of the opinion that the postwar economy, if Keynesian-type demand management policies were to be adopted, would suffer from recurring stop–go problems generated by the 'political business cycle' effect, in contrast to sustained full employment.[5] This state of affairs would mean that governments would be limited in the extent to which they could direct macroeconomic policy to overcome the stagnationist tendencies that Kalecki believed to be inherent in the working of capitalist economies. Only if experience proved able to accommodate or change capitalists' attitudes to interventionism does it seem that this 'political business cycle' effect would be overcome.

In the original version of the paper, though excluded from a later revision (Kalecki 1971). Kalecki concludes with a short discussion concerning the question of whether a 'progressive' should be happy with a regime of political business cycles. He gives two reasons why the answer should be in the negative. First, such a regime will not lead to lasting full employment. It may of course not lead even to transitory periods of full employment if pressure from business and financial interests induces a change in government policy before the economy is operating at full resource capacity. In the context of Kalecki's stagnationist model of capitalist development it is perhaps likely that a prolonged regime of such stop–go attitudes to government deficit spending will lead to a regime of political business cycles around a secularly increasing level of unemployment (although he does not explicitly suggest this). Second, in such a political climate government policy is likely to be limited to public investment activity that avoids any spending that might contribute to the subsidization of consumption. Government investment activity will be further tied to 'the extent to which such investment is *actually needed*' (original emphasis). Hence investment would not be undertaken for general reflationary purposes, but only for the direct benefits that that investment would entail. Kalecki's objection to this state of affairs is that he sees the purpose of economic activity as that of raising the standard of living of the population. So to limit government investment activity to that which is 'actually needed' defeats the use of government policy for redistributive purposes. Hence he concludes that either capitalism must be fundamentally reformed if it is to be enabled to sustain full employment or, if it proves incapable of adjusting to such reforms, it must be replaced.

There has arisen an extensive literature from economists and political scientists on the nature of the relationship between political behaviour and economic policy making. This work largely stems from Nordhaus's (1975) seminal model of an electoral business cycle, a model in which government administrations adjust macroeconomic instruments so as to manipulate macroeconomic variables such as inflation and unemployment in order to maximize the probability of re-election.[6] Given the presumed nature of voters' preferences and effectiveness of policy instruments, the result is a pre-election boom followed by fiscal contraction in the post-election period as inflation starts to accelerate. These models are of course very different from the germ of a theory of the business cycle contained in Kalecki's paper. Locksley (1980) rightly contrasts Kalecki's notion of the political business cycle with these 'orthodox' theories of the electoral business cycle. However the two are not, of course, inconsistent with each other if within the business cycle the desire of capitalists/rentier groups for reflation coincides with the pre-election run-up period. There is of course no reason why this should ever be the case. Given that general elections in democratic market economies occur every four or five years the electoral business cycle approach points to business cycles of a similar time period. As we shall discuss later Kalecki's ideas seem more consistent with longer cycles in economic activity.

Both Locksley (1980) and Borooah (1985) point out that the principal shortcoming of orthodox theories of the electoral business cycle is that they fail to treat the electorate as sectionalized into different groups whose different interests may be at variance with each other. In contrast they tend to adopt the traditional economistic methodology of Tinbergen (1952) and Downs (1957) and view the government as a benign homogeneous entity attempting to maximize the social welfare function of a homogeneous electorate. Individual voters, in this kind of framework, cast their votes in a rational manner for the party that is expected to deliver what

Downs terms the highest 'utility income'. Borooah (1985) makes the point that in a society which is characterized by sectionalized interest groups and where variations in government policy are possible, the role of these interest groups in that society is very important. The ruling political party will manipulate policy so as to favour the groups with which it is most closely allied. However the Kaleckian scenario proceeds further by implicitly asserting that the economic power of capitalists will constrain the activities of any government, be it conservative and allied overtly to capitalist and financial interests or of a left-wing social democratic persuasion and drawing its electoral support predominantly from trades unionists and the employed class.

Alexander (1948) has a rather similar critique of full employment policies under capitalism, applied specifically to the American business community's opposition to proposed deficit spending in the immediate postwar period. Specifically he raises the question of the redistributive consequences of demand management. Feiwel (1974) takes up this argument and makes the point that implicit in Kalecki's discussion is a fourth and most fundamental objection to full employment policies. This is 'the intrinsic apprehension of resulting redistribution of income' (Feiwel 1974, p.33). In other words full employment policies will lead to a 'profits squeeze'.

CONTEMPORARY CONSTRAINTS ON DEMAND MANAGEMENT POLICIES

In this section I wish to investigate arguments for the existence of some contemporary justification for Kalecki's implicit assumption that within the capitalist economy policy is largely conditioned by the desires of capitalist and rentier groups, despite the possibility that these might form an electoral minority.

Cowling (1985) argues persuasively that as economic power becomes more concentrated democracy and capitalism become increasingly incompatible. Within contemporary corporatist capitalism he argues that two forces are at work leading to a growing concentration of economic power at the national level. The first is the asserted growing centralization of power within large business corporations. Undoubtedly large corporations have the potential to exercise considerable economic and political power. In political terms the most obvious manifestation of this is through financial contributions to political parties and through 'consultancy' arrangements with parliamentary representatives. In economic terms large corporations exercise considerable influence on investment and employment through the corporate planning process. However Cowling's point here hinges on the extent to which that power is exercised by a small group of senior individuals. Much play has been made by US and UK governments recently in the assertion of a widespread growth in 'popular capitalism' through increased personal shareholding in companies. In the UK in particular this has been attempted through the tendering to the public of stock in previously state-owned enterprises. Evidence of the growth of individual shareholding through these means is very sparse if not non-existent. It may well be the case that the effect on shareholding concentration within companies has been minimal, particularly if small-scale share purchase has been solely for immediate capital gain. Recent work (Cubbin and Leech 1983, Leech 1987) questions the alleged divorce of ownership and control and uses the analysis of the effects of political voting behaviour to suggest that shareholding concentration, rather than simply whether one individual possesses more than 50 per cent of voting stock, will reflect the extent of ownership control of a corporation. Pitelis and Sugden (1986) develop this argument to suggest that the managerialist perspective dominant in the 1960s was something of a theoretical 'red herring', and that control of today's firms rests with a dominant subset of owners. Similarly the impact of the growth of individual share ownership on control within large corporations may have also been minimal.

The second tendency is that towards the organization of production into transnational corporations. In terms of implications for investment and employment creation and hence indirectly for the efficacy of macroeconomic demand management policies this is potentially more important than the first. The transnational corporation can be viewed as an internal capital market in which investment funds are allocated by a head office to separate production locations around the globe. The 'monopoly capitalism' school sees the growth of transnational corporations as therefore implying a reduction in the importance of international competition in the allocation of capital between nations, supplanted by growing international capital allocation within corporate organizations (Cowling and Sugden 1987). This growth implies a rising international degree of monopoly. This point is of course highly contentious and disputed by other authors who see the role of transnational corporations as one of opening up domestic monopolized markets to the competitive discipline of imports.[7] Auerbach and Skott (1988) argue that growing internationalization of production represents geographical expansion of markets and a widening of the 'domains of competitiveness'. Nevertheless at the local level the impact of a change in the investment activities of transnational corporations can lead to economic stagnation.[8]

It seems reasonable to suggest that the international flow of investment funds as directed by transnational corporations will be conditioned by economic and political conditions within prospective host nations. If those responsible for capital allocation find the economic policy stance unacceptable in country X then production will be relocated elsewhere. Furthermore internal pricing mechanisms operating within transnational corporations allow the controllers of those organizations to accrue profit where it is most advantageous for them to do so. Hence elected policy makers in country X, in order to maintain the economic advantages derived from acting as host for a transnational's production facility, will be forced to adopt a policy stance acceptable to the transnational's head office. And, of course, for exactly the reasons identified by Kalecki these global capitalists might insist on 'sound finance' and non-interventionism to maintain labour discipline and avoid any perceived spoiling of markets. Furthermore they might also require the payment of investment incentives and the favourable tax treatment of profits. This conditionality in the flow of investment may present elected policy makers with the dilemma of following the wishes of their constituents or promoting policies favourable to foreign investment. A dilemma would exist if the two are at odds with each other. Cowling clearly sees this to be the case:

> while we might expect the advent of universal suffrage to lead to demands for the redistribution of income, wealth and power in favour of the majority, the existence of giant transnational centres of economic power will undermine such

democratic demands. Indeed we can see the growth of transnationalism as partly a response to the problems posed . . . by the advent of greater political democracy. (Cowling 1985, p. 240)

Elsewhere he and Roger Sugden go on to argue that such a process will exacerbate stagnationary forces within the economic system, as transnational corporations play one nation off against another for increased profits in what amounts to a global version of the Kalecki–Steindl theory of stagnation (Cowling and Sugden 1987).

On a more contentious note Cowling allies declining economic democracy with rising concentration of economic power in the mass communications industries of printing and broadcasting. He cites Hirsch and Gordon (1975) who argue that the pursuit of profit within these industries leads to excessive attention being paid to the interests of more affluent groups. This is because these groups are the ones to which advertising expenditures are most fruitfully directed.

Pertinent to this view are questions concerning the way in which ideas concerning the appropriateness of differing economic policy options are disseminated to the electorate and the way in which the electorate's perceptions about economic problems can be shifted. For example Borooah (1985) argues that unemployment is only perceived as a serious economic problem if it is rising. Presumably this is because the individual voter then perceives more acutely the risk of his or her own unemployment. On the other hand, citing the evidence of Daniel (1975), he suggests that perceptions about inflation as a problem are stable. Inflation affects all individuals engaged in economic transactions. Unemployment, on the other hand, has a greater effect on certain identifiable groups. For example during the crisis experienced by the British economy in the early 1980s the greater effect of unemployment was particularly felt by the young and the unskilled. Discussion and criticism of inflation may be more keenly disseminated to the electorate than discussion of unemployment through the media. This will be so if those media perceive inflation to be a more pressing threat to their own interests, or to the interests of a greater proportion of their viewers, listeners or readers.

Indeed we might argue that the Conservative party in Britain has in recent years sought to maintain voters' perceptions about the effects and dangers of inflation whilst trying to avoid any appeal to its perceptions about the problems of unemployment and deficient aggregate demand. Hence for a government facing the kind of dominant economic paradigm identified by Kalecki, the pursuit of a reflationary policy may be politically much more difficult than the pursuit of one of deflation or non-intervention. The re-emergence of inflationary tendencies in the British economy in the second half of 1988 and 1989 has reasserted the control of inflation as the overriding economic objective of the Conservative government, who perceive the problem as remaining of crucial political importance.

A POSTWAR POLITICO-ECONOMIC 'LONG WAVE'?

Although Kalecki, almost as an afterthought, suggests that capitalists' ambivalence to reflationary public expenditure will produce a political business cycle, it seems that the kind of political and social changes resulting from a prolonged period of full employment are only likely to take place over the medium or long term. Despite the evidence of, for example, Boddy and Crotty (1975) and Weisskopf (1979) on the cyclical effect of tight labour markets on profitability, it is difficult to conceive of major shifts in the political balance of power between workers and capitalist groups taking place within the limited time period of a conventional business cycle. If we take this view then it seems that some of the problems Kalecki associates with the maintenance of full employment may only emerge in the medium or long term.

Table 8.1 presents decade averages of growth rates since 1951 and manufacturing profit rates since 1971 for five of the major OECD economies. These demonstrate the slowdown in economic growth from the 1970s. In all cases and especially in those of the UK and USA the profit rate averages hide the sustained progressive revival in profitability since 1981. The lower two sections of the table present similar averages for two major labour market performance indicators, namely rates of unemployment and working days lost through strikes. The unemployment figures demonstrate the progressive worsening of unemployment in all of the economies since the 1960s, although the rise is of course very slight in the case of Japan. The interesting impressionistic information on a long cycle in worker militancy emerges from the figures for working days lost through strikes. A common pattern

Table 8.1   Rates of growth, profit, unemployment and strike activity in major OECD economies 1951–1987

	USA	Canada	Japan	UK	W.Germany
i Average annual rate of growth of real GDP (%)					
1951–60	3.3	4.1	8.3[a]	2.7	7.8
1961–70	4.0	5.1	10.7	2.9	4.9
1971–80	2.8	4.5	5.2	1.9	2.7
1981–87	3.0	3.1	3.8	2.3	1.4
ii Average annual manufacturing net rate of profit (%)					
1951–60	n.a.	n.a.	n.a.	n.a.	n.a.
1961–70	n.a.	n.a.	n.a.	n.a.	n.a.
1971–80	19.1	14.3	25.5[b]	7.6	16.5
1981–87	13.9	9.7[c]	19.8[b]	6.6	14.1[d]
iii Average annual total unemployment rate (%)					
1951–60	4.5	4.5	1.4	1.6	5.2
1961–70	4.7	5.0	1.0	2.1	1.0
1971–80	6.4	6.9	1.8	4.6	3.1
1981–87	7.7	10.1	2.6	11.3	8.3
iv Average annual million working days lost through strikes					
1951–60	32.3	1.7	6.0	3.4	1.0
1961–70	32.3	3.6	3.8	4.4	0.3
1971–80	32.1	7.6	4.2	13.0	1.2
1981–87	10.8	5.3	0.4	7.5	0.8

[a] 1953–60 average
[b] gross manufacturing rate of profit
[c] 1981–84 average
[d] 1981–85 average
Sources: i and ii: OECD National Accounts, various years iii and iv: International Labour Office, *Yearbook of Labour Statistics*, various years.

is that strike intensity has risen in the 1960s and 1970s and begun to fall back in the 1980s, coincident with the rise in unemployment and the revival in profitability. These figures offer far from final evidence of a long cycle of worker militancy coincident with trends in growth and profitability and conceal much detail. However they may portray an impression of this.

Kalecki's assertion that full employment maintenance would require increasing government budget deficits was not proved correct in the 1950s and 1960s. As Matthews (1968) points out the decline in unemployment in the 20 years following the Second World War was not a Keynesian phenomenon. Governments of both the Left and the Right in the UK consistently ran budget surpluses during this time. Government expenditures as a proportion of national income rose but these were more than matched by rising tax revenues. Matthews attributes this virtuous circle to an upward shift in the aggregate investment function of the British economy, induced by a belief among capitalists that governments would and could prevent a slump. In his words there was a widespread belief in a 'safety net theory of the role of government'. So the short-run cyclical changes in capitalists' attitude to government deficits suggested by Kalecki appear not to have materialized. Nevertheless it seems that if we consider the postwar period as a whole it is only in the late 1960s and 1970s that major shifts in the social and political consciousness of the working class start to present serious problems of 'labour discipline'. During the 1950s and 1960s, particularly in the USA, massive military expenditures associated with the Korean War and later Vietnam, combined with buoyant tax revenues resulting from a prolonged period of economic growth, preserved the capitalist system from serious cyclical crises while at the same time avoiding the objectionable consequences of governments' straying into the 'subsidization of mass consumption' and large-scale intervention into the workings of *'laissez-faire'*.

In the 1943 paper Kalecki suggests that the armaments expenditure unleashed by the Fascist regimes in the Europe of the 1930s provided one, though to him a wholly unacceptable, solution to the political problems of aggregate demand maintenance. Hence he viewed the armaments build-up during the Cold War and later the proliferation of the war in Vietnam in a similar vein[9] – one solution to the problem of generating markets for industrial production but not a solution that would benefit the standard of living of the general population. Feiwel somewhat heroically suggests that perhaps Kalecki appears to have suffered from what he calls the 'Einstein syndrome':

> Having shown (together with Keynes) to the capitalist world how it could save (and reform) itself by relieving (and in some sense doing away with) periodic depression, this world seems to have turned insane, for instead of raising the standard of living to a higher level than that achieved so far by public investment, resources were being wasted in armaments production and periodic small-scale wars that turned into large-scale disasters. (Feiwel 1974, p. 35)

So why did the sustained economic growth of the 1950s and 1960s come to an end, to be eventually replaced after the crises of the early and mid-1970s with the monetarist 'experiment' and latterly with what appears to be a more pragmatic approach to policy generally informed by a new-classical macroeconomic analysis? The reasons for the breakdown in the economic efficacy of Keynesian policies and the Phillips curve relationship in the late 1960s and early 1970s have, of course, been much discussed elsewhere.[10] But drawing on the ideas of Kalecki's 1943 paper we can perhaps highlight a number of additional, though not mutually inconsistent and certainly not complete, explanations.

First, it is clear from the history of the late 1960s that, to use Kalecki's phrase, the 'social position of the boss' was perceived as being under threat and that the working-class and trade union movement did start to assume increased levels of militancy. In the USA the 20-year period from the late 1940s through to the late 1960s is often characterized as the period of capital–labour accord or in less optimistic terms 'accommodation' (Bowles et al. 1983, 1986, Edwards and Podgursky 1986). The pattern for this accord was set by developments in collective bargaining in the automobile industry in the late 1940s, which established the long-term (three-year) employment contracts specifying a two-stage wage-setting process of 'cost of living adjustment' and 'annual improvement factor'. The former effectively established a real wage norm (Perry 1980) and the latter established a norm for the distribution of gains from productivity improvements. The establishment of 'pattern bargaining' enabled coordination of agreements within and between industries. The *quid pro quo* of this arrangement was the assurance of management control over decision making (Bowles et al. 1986). In the 1970s this accommodation began to break down. Edwards and Podgursky (1986) identify a number of microeconomic reasons hinging on the reduced ability of employers to shield themselves behind oligopolistic market power from the rising real wages that the accord entailed. Rising import competition and deregulation increased product market competition and increased competition from non-unionized sectors. At the macroeconomic level rising inflation and stagnation placed employers under greater pressure to cut costs and revive flagging profit rates. On the trade union side Mitchell (1985) identifies an upward shift in the wage 'norm' accompanied by rising militancy and strike action. The effect was therefore to bring back into focus the latent employer–employee distributional conflict that was suppressed during the period of 'accommodation'.

In the UK there existed no such accord as developed in the USA, except perhaps during the period of the postwar Labour Government of 1945 to 1951. During this period it is usually argued that the wage–cost–push inflationary consequences of full employment policies were prevented because of the restraint exercised by trades unions during the immediate postwar period of reconstruction (Balogh 1982, Phelps-Brown 1983). During the 1950s and early 1960s, though, conditions of sustained economic growth may also have diverted distributional conflict. The Council on Prices, Productivity and Incomes stated in 1961:

The total of wages and salaries paid out by companies was very nearly doubled in only nine years, from 1950 to 1959, but meanwhile these companies' gross profits (after allowing for stock appreciation) were likewise very nearly doubled. The constancy of proportion is the general rule: . . . other western countries have experienced it too. It is highly significant for policy. Rises in pay have not been coming out of profits. When firms find that in practice they can maintain profits despite negotiating pay rises that increase their costs, and that they can maintain sales despite raising their selling prices, the restraints of the market are removed. (Council on Prices, Productivity and Incomes 1961, quoted by Phelps-Brown 1983)

By the mid- to late 1960s these conditions no longer held. Britain, in particular, experienced a rapid rise in trade union membership during the period of the late 1960s and 1970s (a rise which has since been rapidly reversed). The evidence of Chapters 6 and 7 supports, along with other authors (Martin 1978, Kilpatrick and Lawson 1980, Wolff 1986), the theory that the secular decline in profitability can be explained by inflationary pressure on real wages outstripping productivity growth. This has been advanced for both the USA and the UK. In the context of these sorts of problems a dose of unemployment and period of reduced government intervention in the management of the economy to slacken inflationary pressure in labour markets may well have seemed attractive to certain interest groups (Locksley 1978).

Second, the maintenance of demand management required new outlets for government spending activity and therefore increased interventionism. The American extrication from Vietnam and replacement of Cold War policies with 'détente' in the 1970s obviated the need for continued armaments investment from particularly the US government. Kalecki's reasoning would lead to the conclusion that if Keynesian-type fiscal management were to continue it would require a redirection of government spending into activities that capitalists would dislike. This would lead to pressure for a change of policy. In Britain the period from the end of the Second World War to the mid-1970s was of course marked by increased government interventionism, not only at the level of macroeconomic management, but also at the microeconomic level. In particular the three periods of Labour government during this time saw programmes of nationalization – a development Kalecki explicitly mentions in the 1943 paper. Also the absence of prolonged periods of social consensus over the vexing question of income distribution led to increased inflationary pressure (Balogh 1982). In turn this led, particularly in Britain and to a lesser extent in the USA, to increased government control over prices and incomes removing the freedom of both capitalists and trades unions alike to determine for themselves the price of their products. Attempts to restore some sort of distributional norm by patching together a 'social contract' between government, unions and capitalists in the mid-1970s failed. The Labour Government's voluntarist approach to incomes policy begun in late 1974 broke down in 1978 and 1979 in the face of rising wage inflation and strike activity.

Finally we can consider the effect of rising inflationary pressure on the financial sector. Bhaduri and Steindl (1985) argue that Keynesian policies threatened the social position of the financial sector since they entailed 'an enormous strengthening of the national government's hand in the conduct of banking policy'. Monetarism arose as a social doctrine, they argue, because a return to restrictive monetary, and therefore accommodatingly tight fiscal, policies would reverse this effect by lowering inflationary pressure and hence reducing the erosion of the value of financial assets and allowing the restoration of profitable high interest rates. The usual associated disadvantages of restrictive national credit policies could be circumvented by international banks operating in the global capital market. From the mid- and late 1970s the huge growth of the extranational Eurodollar market particularly facilitated this.

So if we take a Kaleckian line there would appear to have been a certain political inevitability in the dawning of an anti-Keynesian backlash in the leading capitalist economies in the late 1970s. To quote Kalecki once more:

In this situation a powerful block is likely to be formed between big business and the *rentier* interests, and they would probably find more than one economist to declare that the situation was manifestly unsound. The pressure of all these forces, and in particular of big business would probably induce the Government to return to the orthodox policy of cutting down the budget deficit. (Kalecki 1943, p.330, author's emphasis)

By the 1970s a large number of economists particularly in the USA had joined the lone voice of Friedman to argue for the benefits of monetary and fiscal restraint, and to point out the unsoundness of growing deficit spending.[11] Monetarism, if it was ever implemented in an ideologically pure form (Smith 1987), soon gave way, particularly in the UK, to a more pragmatic form of anti-Keynesianism, which exalts a commitment to 'principles of sound finance'.

The other aspect of the anti-Keynesianism of the early 1980s was the use of unemployment to curb the effect of trades unions on wage demands. In both the USA and the UK the political and legal environment swung sharply against trade union activity. After the stagflationary crisis of the 1970s there has been much discussion of the 1980s heralding permanent changes in the balance of bargaining power between capital and labour. This is particularly so in the USA where work by the Brookings Institution points to a drop in union wage 'norm' in the 1980s, as union representation and strike activity have fallen (Mitchell 1985). This may also have been accompanied by a change in trend towards a narrowing of the union–non-union wage mark-up. There has been much recent discussion by industrial relations specialists of permanent changes in the American industrial relations system, symptomatic of considerable weakening in the collective strength of labour (Piore and Sabel 1984, Edwards and Podgursky 1986). Indeed in many sectors of American industry employers have adopted overt strategies to speed the emergence of a non-unionized industrial relations system (Kochan, Katz and McKersie 1986).

In the UK the 1980s have seen the enactment of a series of legislation explicitly designed to redress the alleged imbalance of power between capital and labour. In macroeconomic terms this was seen as an important element of supply-side policies to curb wage inflation.[12] It was also motivated in more general terms as a precondition for the re-establishment of competitive conditions in the labour market and so included measures such as limiting strike action by workers to disputes at their own workplace, and the requirement of secret ballots to sanction strike action, elect union leaders and sanction closed shop arrangements. At the same time the 1980s have seen a sharp reduction in trade union membership, though this was probably in the short term largely the result of rising unemployment and general economic recession, rather than any direct effect of legislative change on the perceived benefits of union membership (Carruth and Disney 1988).

THE PROSPECTS FOR A FUTURE RETURN TO FULL EMPLOYMENT

Kalecki's important contribution in his 1943 paper was to suggest that prolonged periods of full employment may prove politically unacceptable in class-sectionalized capitalist societies. Indeed it would seem that if one takes a long perspective on the postwar economic history of some of the major industrialized economies that Kalecki has to some extent been eventually proved correct.

The logic of the scenario portrayed above leads on to the suggestion that conventional 'demand-side' macroeconomic solutions to current high levels of unemployment in economies such as the UK may prove very difficult to make effective. This is despite the fact that careful stimulation of economic growth will reduce government expenditure commitments on 'stabilizers' such as unemployment benefit and social security provision and that, as we are currently observing, growing aggregate demand leads to growing tax receipts. Indeed in the UK, as far as we can tell, the current Conservative government perceives large-scale reflationary public expenditure policy as anathema to British business interests for mainly similar reasons as those suggested by Kalecki. This commitment however has not ruled out, on either side of the Atlantic, the pursuit of expansionary tax-cutting fiscal policy justified on the grounds of supply-side reform.

It does seem that the current prolonged period of high unemployment being experienced particularly in the UK is inertial, which suggests that, were a wider-reaching change in attitude to fiscal reflation to come about, then the political constraints identified by Kalecki would start to 'bind' very quickly. First, the period since about 1982 has seen considerable scrapping of excess capacity and restructuring of British industry (Wadhwani and Wall 1986). As capitalists operating in Britain began to realize that the depression of 1979 was not to be swiftly followed by a reflation then it became rational to reduce excess capacity rather than hold it. Unprofitable unplanned excess capacity generates a strong motive on the part of capitalists for demands for aggregate demand stimulation. As much of this capacity has now been scrapped, this motive is severely weakened. Reflation may lead quickly to distributional conflict. One of the key points to emerge from Chapter 7 was that the recent prolonged revival in UK corporate profitability has come about because expansion has been sustained for a much longer than usual period of time without the onset of the mid-expansion pressure on profit share. Indeed the profitability revival may mean that business interests perceive little need for further demand-led attempts to reduce unemployment, notwith-standing the other macroeconomic difficulties which such a policy would at the time of writing generate. In any case, in the light of restored high levels of capacity utilization, fiscal expansion may result in considerably more price adjustment and inflationary pressure than would have been the case five years ago. Such inflationary pressure would surely soon arouse the dislike of the financial sector as Bhaduri and Steindl suggest was the case in the 1970s.

Second, a number of economists have recently argued that the European economies, and particularly the UK, seem prone to sustained unemployment persistence (Blanchard and Summers 1986). This phenomenon has come to be described by the term labour market 'hysteresis', and is in general terms characterized by an unresponsiveness of wage bargainers to changes in external economic conditions.[13] Principally two mechanisms have been suggested as being important in generating unemployment persistence. The first identifies the atrophication of the human capital of unemployed workers as their unemployment duration lengthens. As unemployed workers remain unemployed they cease to exercise a competitive discipline on wage setting. In Marxian terms the reserve army ceases effectively to discipline wage demands. The second mechanism highlights the importance of the distinction between 'insiders' of the labour market and 'outsiders' (Solow 1985, Lindbeck and Snower 1986), and essentially represents a more rigorous formulation of ideas concerning labour market segmentation. The commonest conception of this is to identify skilled unionized workers as insiders. In a recession some insiders lose their jobs and therefore their insider status. When demand conditions improve again the remaining insider group prefer to renegotiate their share of the monopolistic bargaining surplus in terms of higher wages rather than increased employment. Under such conditions labour discipline among labour market 'insiders' would start to break down much more quickly than might be suggested by a cursory glance at usual summary statistics on unemployment. Insider–outsider models therefore provide an explanation for the isolation of wage and employment determination from external economic conditions. The consequence of hysteresis for the effectiveness of Keynesian reflationary policies is severe. Any government-initiated stimulus to labour demand is likely to result in wage adjustment rather than employment adjustment. This is perhaps illustrated by the behaviour of unemployment and wage inflation in the UK recently. The sustained upswing since 1982 that as shown in Chapter 7 has brought about a steady growth in the rate of profit has been characterized by considerable real wage growth (Table 7.8) at a time of a record level of unemployment, which at least until 1985 was showing little downward movement. Problems associated with hysteresis do not appear to be prevalent in the USA (Blanchard and Summers 1986). This may be because the power of trades unions in the UK was not as seriously eroded by the crisis of the 1970s as in the USA and, despite the Conservative government's programme of employment legislation, has remained effective in the 1980s.

Finally the increased internationalization of capital markets (both external and internal to corporations), in conjunction with contemporary commitment to some degree of floating exchange rates, means that 'capital flight' may now pose an increasingly serious problem for governments intent on a unilateralist reflationary strategy. Indeed the experiences of France under the Mitterand administration of the early 1980s and the USA under its 1987 budget deficit crisis bear this out.

The approach of this chapter has been a broad brush one and consequently rather sketchy. Indeed the issues it covers merit several volumes in themselves. In particular there is clearly a need to substantiate many of the points raised by more thorough future research. Any conclusions drawn must of necessity therefore be tentative and imprecise. Accepting Feiwel's point that at the heart of Kalecki's analysis of the problems of reflationary public expenditure is the question of capitalism's capacity to deal adequately with the problem of income distribution under full employment then two alternatives are possible. Either the capitalist economy must develop effective institutional mechanisms to achieve consensus over the distribution of income under full employment or a return to the prolonged conditions of full employment enjoyed during the 1950s and 1960s will remain infeasible. In the latter case the prediction is made even gloomier by the possibility that, with growing labour market hysteresis, an equilibrium distribution of income (bargained division of wages and profits) under which stable prices (or rate of increase of prices) can be maintained may require higher and higher accommodating levels of unemployment. In the former case there is little from the past British or American experience of attempts to maintain stability under full employment using incomes policies to suggest much future hope. In this respect lasting social consensus on distribution may well be conditional on more innovative attempts at designing the institutional framework under which collective bargaining is conducted.[14]

NOTES

1. This chapter contains a revised and extended version of material that previously appeared as Henley (1988b).
2. Kalecki's original 1943 article is reprinted as pp. 420–430 of Hunt and Schwartz (1972) and in an abridged form as pp. 138–145 of Kalecki (1971).
3. He based this on attitudes of big business to government spending in interwar economies such as during the US New Deal, the Blum experiment in France and the experience of pre-Nazi Germany.
4. Kalecki's work hence fits in with the ideas of American stagnationist Keynesians such as Domar and Hansen (e.g. Domar 1946). The similarity between the Keynesian and Kaleckian analysis of the problem of inadequate effective demand is often noted. However the two approaches differ in that for Keynes and early British Keynesians the problem was one of attempting to employ demand management policies to correct periodic deviations from full employment and maintain the level of aggregate demand. Kalecki, on the other hand, stressed the importance of a long-run deficit policy or policy of income redistribution to redress these stagnationist tendencies and maintain a stable level of aggregate demand. He was, for example, critical of the 1944 White Paper on Employment Policy for failing to recognize this aspect of policy (Sawyer 1985).
5. Alexander (1948) also expresses similar doubts about the long-term efficacy of (then) prospective postwar demand management policies in the USA.
6. A good review of such models is provided by Locksley (1980). See also Frey and Schneider (1975), Wagner (1977) and MacRae (1977).
7. The conditions under which imports may or may not act as a competitive discipline on domestic producers is investigated by Geroski and Jacquemin (1981). Caves (1982) provides a survey of the effect of foreign direct investment on competition.
8. For example the impact of transnational disinvestment in the West Midlands of the UK is graphically detailed in Gaffikin and Nickson (1984).
9. Kalecki deals with this in a series of papers reproduced posthumously in Kalecki (1972), in particular 'Stimulating the Business Upswing in Nazi Germany' (1935), 'The Economic Situation in the United States as Compared with the Pre-War Period' (1956) and 'The Fascism of Our Times' (1964).

10. For example in Skidelsky (1977) and Dean (1981).
11. Two important voices in this respect are James Buchanan and Richard E. Wagner, who articulated the 'evils' of Keynesianism in their influential book *Democracy in Deficit* (1977) in the USA, and in the UK through their Institute of Economic Affairs paper 'The Consequences of Mr. Keynes' (1978).
12. A prominent exposition of this argument is to be found in Minford (1983).
13. Cross (1988) provides a collection of recent papers on labour market hysteresis.
14. One example might be found in profit-sharing arrangements. Recent work by Weitzman (1983, 1984) and Meade (1986) suggests that profit sharing has the potential to provide the economy with greater macroeconomic stability. This suggestion has already provoked considerable academic debate and invites more thorough empirical investigation. However it is perhaps of no coincidence that those economies, such as Japan, West Germany and Sweden, that have weathered the 1980s world recession much better than the UK from the point of view of maintaining employment all have long-established employee participation mechanisms and arrangements for profit sharing.

9. Conclusion

The role of industrial structure and of collective bargaining strength in the determination of wages and profits provides a key link between industrial organization and the macroeconomy. The discussion in the present book has fallen into two halves. In the first half we have addressed the microeconomic question of how the degree of monopolistic power in the markets, both in final product markets and in the market for the labour input, influences profitability and the division of income generated by production between those profits and wage income. In the second half of the book we have gone on to examine secular and cyclical movements in aggregate profitability at the macroeconomic level for the US and UK economies. In the broadest possible terms we conclude from this second half of the book that we can observe secular and particularly cyclical movements in the components of the aggregate profit rate, notably in the distribution of income, that are quite inconsistent with the operation of competitive markets.

Increasingly both labour and industrial economists are coming to view trade union collective bargaining activity and producer market power as complementary explanations for, in the labour economists' case, wage and employment determination and for, in the industrial economists' case, profit margins and rates of return. It is becoming clear that we tend to observe a significant union–non-union wage differential only where we observe the presence of a significant monopolistic surplus for which union negotiators can compete. That monopolistic surplus is only likely to exist where we observe a high level of market concentration, perhaps buttressed by the absence of the disciplining effect of competitive foreign import penetration. Both the inter-industry wage share equations estimated by other authors and those results reported in Chapter 3 provide evidence of the average effects of product market power and union bargaining strength. Behind those averages may hide a story of both competitive industries where there is no surplus and therefore no union impact and of oligopolistic industries which in turn offer considerable scope for collective bargaining activity to push for the redistribution of product market rents towards workers.

However the time dimension is crucial to this picture. This is because the ability of firms to create and maintain sizeable profit margins is dependent on aggregate demand conditions in the economy and therefore on the currently observed position in the business cycle. In the initial stages of a business upswing the oligopolistic firm is able to enjoy improved demand conditions by improved utilization of capacity. Consequently its rate of profit increases. At the same time conditions of rising demand allow cost increases to be passed easily on into higher final prices. As the upswing progresses this ability to pass on costs becomes more limited. Buoyant macroeconomic conditions impart bargaining strength to trades unions, but because capacity utilization is reaching its peak wage demands cannot be matched by further improvements in productivity. At this point union impact on profits is perhaps greatest but is likely to be short-lived. Profit margins begin to fall, in turn stimulating greater rivalry for market share between oligopolistic protagonists. When the downswing comes demand conditions worsen, profits fall and rising unemployment limits the capacity of unions to stake their claim to the diminishing surplus.

We cannot very adequately measure concepts like union bargaining strength and oligopolistic rivalry, and comprehensive time series of measures of proxy variables such as trade union membership and industrial concentration are difficult, if not impossible, to obtain. In general we can only over time observe their effects. The cyclical analysis for the USA and UK presented in Chapters 6 and 7 is very consistent with the explanation presented above. A critical feature of the typical American or British business cycle is the premature peak in profitability, which comes about because real wage growth in the closing stages of the upswing outstrips that of real productivity.

Over the span of the several business cycles that have occurred in both the American and British economies since the Second World

War it is quite difficult to identify specific trends in the influence of trade union power and in product market monopoly power. The 'monopoly capitalism' school seeks to argue that contemporary capitalism will *ceteris paribus* be characterized by the growing influence of product market monopolization, and in turn that this trend will lead to declining capacity utilization, profitability and as a result to stagnant investment and poor economic growth. Although generally upward over the long time span of the twentieth century trends in concentration move very slowly. In the postwar period perhaps the 1950s and 1960s stand out as a time of rising concentration, especially in the UK. This period also experienced rising profit margins and redistribution away from, in particular, production worker wage income. However during this period economic growth was very good in comparison with the two decades that were to follow. The 1970s and 1980s have in stark contrast witnessed for the USA and the UK the growing discipline of foreign import competition. Yet, for reasons that probably have little to do with secular trends towards a more concentrated industrial structure, the 1970s and early 1980s experienced the conditions of stagnation and inflation that the monopoly capital approach would have predicted.

Nevertheless to repeat the point, the cyclical behaviour of profits and distribution is markedly different from that which we might expect to be generated by a more competitive industrial structure. The 'degree of monopoly' changes considerably over the cycle, and one important reason for this is that the cycle sees considerable changes in trade union strength. This instability in profitability must, through its influence on investment, in turn contribute to the fluctuations in economic activity which are prevalent within advanced capitalist economies such as the UK and USA.

The hostile attitude towards trade union activity from British policy makers since 1979, combined with a reluctance to adopt the overt use of demand management policies to limit the extent of economic recession has succeeded in postponing the usual mid-expansion peak in profitability. In part this may simply be because the level of unemployment in the early 1980s in the UK was so high that trade union capacity to influence the division of the bargaining surplus was so low. This postponement might have occurred regardless of the increased tightening of the legal framework governing industrial relations. At the time of writing a resurgence of trade union militancy over pay issues, in the face of rising inflation, might indicate that the Thatcher revolution has done little to affect the future cyclical instability of profitability.

Traditional Keynesian approaches have tended to avoid important microeconomic issues about the supply-side structure of the economy, favouring policies to make the national 'cake' bigger if conflict over the size of the 'slices' creates macroeconomic difficulties. An alternative analysis would stress the importance of the supply-side structural problems, particularly those relating to the industrial price-setting behaviour. This is in contrast to the rationale behind the recent policy stance. The focus of policy makers on both sides of the Atlantic in the 1980s has largely been towards the trade union side of the balance of power in the labour market, paying little more than lip service to the product market. Existing anti-trust policies may help to maintain the status quo, preventing unfettered moves towards higher industrial concentration. However deregulation and privatization of public utilities may exacerbate the problems associated with monopolistic price-setting behaviour. In this context supply-side reforms in the labour market may, as we have argued is currently the case in the UK, postpone rather than eradicate the macroeconomic problems associated with the monopolistic behaviour observed within both labour and product markets. Only policies designed to deal with both will serve to redress the balance of power towards the demand side of the product market.

Bibliography

Addison, J.T. (1983), 'The evolving debate on unions and productivity', *Journal of Industrial Relations*, vol. 25, pp. 286-300.

Addison, J.T. and Hirsch, B.T. (1989), 'Union effects on productivity, profits and growth: has the long run arrived?', *Journal of Labor Economics*, vol. 7, pp. 72-105.

Alexander, S.S. (1948), 'Opposition to deficit spending for the prevention of unemployment', in Metzler .A. et al. (eds), *Essays in Honour of Alvin H. Hansen*, New York, Norton.

Arrow, K.J. and Hahn, F.H. (1971), *General Competitive Analysis*, Edinburgh, Oliver and Boyd.

Asimakopulos, A. (1975), 'A Kaleckian theory of income distribution', *Canadian Journal of Economics*, vol. 8, pp. 313-333.

Auerbach, P. and Skott, P. (1988), 'Concentration, competition and distribution – a critique of theories of monopoly capital', *International Review of Applied Economics*, vol. 2, pp. 42-61.

Bacon, R. and Eltis, W. (1978), *Britain's Economic Problem: Too Few Producers*, 2nd edn, London, Macmillan.

Bain, J.S. (1951), 'Relation of profit rate to industry concentration in American manufacturing 1936-1940', *Quarterly Journal of Economics*, vol. 65, pp. 293-324.

Balogh, T. (1982), *The Irrelevance of Conventional Economics*, London, Weidenfeld and Nicolson.

Baran, P.A. and Sweezy, P.M. (1966), *Monopoly Capital*, New York, Monthly Review Press.

Barbee, W.C. (1974), 'An inquiry into the relationship between market concentration and labor's share of value added', unpublished Ph.D. dissertation, Catholic University of America, Washington, D.C.

Barber, R. and Rifkin, J. (1978), *The North Will Rise Again: Pensions, Politics and Power in the 1980's*, Boston, Beacon Press.

Basile, L. and Salvadori, N. (1984), 'Kalecki's pricing theory', *Journal of Post-Keynesian Economics*, vol. 7, pp. 249–262.

Bauer, P. (1942), 'A note on monopoly', *Economica*, vol. 8, pp. 194–202.

Baumol, W.J., Panzar, J. and Willig, R.D. (1982), *Contestable Markets and the Theory of Industrial Structure*, New York, Harcourt Brace Jovanovitch.

Becker, G.S. (1964), *Human Capital*, Princeton University Press.

Berg, S.A. (1986), 'Excess capacity and the degree of collusion: the Norwegian experience, 1967–82', *International Journal of Industrial Organization*, vol. 4, pp. 99–108.

Bhaduri, A. and Steindl, J. (1985), 'The rise of monetarism as a social doctrine', in Arestis, P. and Skouras, T., *Post-Keynesian Economic Theory: A Challenge to Neoclassical Economics*, Brighton, Wheatsheaf.

Bils, M. (1987), 'The cyclical behaviour of marginal cost and price', *American Economic Review*, vol. 77, pp. 838–855.

Blanchard, O.J. (1987), 'Aggregate and individual price adjustment', *Brookings Papers on Economic Activity*, no. 1, pp. 57–109.

Blanchard, O.J. and Fischer, S. (1989), *Lectures on Macroeconomics*, Cambridge, MA, MIT Press.

Blanchard, O.J. and Kiyotaki, N. (1987), 'Monopolistic competition and the effects of aggregate demand', *American Economic Review*, Vol. 77, pp. 647–666.

Blanchard O.J. and Summers, L.H. (1986), 'Hysteresis and the European Unemployment Problem' in S. Fischer (ed.), *NBER Macroeconomics Annual*, Cambridge MA, MIT Press, also reprinted in Cross (1988).

Bleaney, M. (1976), *Underconsumption Theories: A History and Critical Assessment*, London, Lawrence and Wishart.

Bliss, C.J. (1975), *Capital Theory and the Distribution of Income*, Amsterdam, North-Holland.

Bobel, I. (1978), *Industrial Organisation*, Tubingen, Demokrit Verlag.

Boddy, R. and Crotty, J. (1975), 'Class conflict and macro-policy:

the political business cycle', *Review of Radical Political Economics*, Spring, pp. 1–19.

Borooah, V. (1985), 'The interaction between economic policy and political performance', in R.C.O. Matthews (ed.), *Economy and Democracy*, London, Macmillan.

Bowers, J., Deaton, D. and Turk, J. (1982), *Labour Hoarding in British Industries*, Oxford, Basil Blackwell.

Bowles, S., Gordon, D.M. and Weisskopf, T.E. (1983), *Beyond the Wasteland: A Democratic Alternative to Economic Decline*, New York, Anchor Press/Doubleday.

Bowles, S., Gordon, D.M. and Weisskopf, T.E. (1986), 'Power and profits: the social structure of accumulation and the profitability of the post-war US economy', *Review of Radical Political Economics*, vol. 18, pp. 132–167.

Brack, J. (1987), 'Price adjustment within a framework of symmetric oligopoly: an analysis of pricing in 380 U.S. manufacturing industries, 1958–71', *International Journal of Industrial Organization*, vol. 5, pp. 289–301.

Brack, J. and Cowling, K. (1983), 'Advertising and labour supply: workweek and workyear in U.S. manufacturing industries 1919–76', *Kyklos*, vol. 36, pp. 285–303.

Braverman, H. (1974), *Labor and Monopoly Capital*, New York, Monthly Review Press.

Breusch, T.S. and Pagan, A.R. (1979), 'A simple test for heteroskedasticity and random coefficient variation', *Econometrics*, vol. 47, pp. 1287–1294.

Brown, W. (1981), *The Changing Contours of British Industrial Relations: A Survey of Manufacturing Industry*, Oxford, Basil Blackwell.

Brush, B.C. and Crane, S.E. (1984), 'Wage share, market power and unionism: some contrary U.S. evidence', *Manchester School*, vol. 52, pp. 613–639.

Buchanan, J.M. and Wagner, R.E. (1977), *Democracy in Deficit: The Political Legacy of Lord Keynes*, New York, Academic Press.

Buchanan, J.M., Burton, J. and Wagner, R.E. (1978), *The Consequences of Mr Keynes*, Institute of Economic Affairs, Hobart Paper No. 78.

Burgess, G.J. and Webb, A.J. (1974), 'Rates of return and profit shares in the United Kingdom', *Lloyds Bank Review*, April.

Burns, A.F. and Mitchell, W.C. (1946), *Measuring Business Cycles*, New York, National Bureau of Economic Research.

Carruth, A.A. and Disney, R.F. (1988), 'Where have two million trade union members gone?', *Economica*, vol, 55, pp. 1–20.

Caves, R.E. (1982), *Multinational Enterprise and Economic Analysis*, Cambridge, Cambridge University Press.

Caves, R.E. (1985), 'International trade and industrial organization: problems, solved and unsolved', *European Economic Review*, vol. 28, pp. 377–395.

Chamberlin, E.H. (1933), *The Theory of Monopolistic Competition*, Cambridge, MA., Harvard University Press.

Clarke, R. (1985), *Industrial Economics*, Oxford, Blackwell.

Clarke, R., Davies, S.W. and Waterson, M. (1984), 'The profitability–concentration relation: market power or efficiency?', *Journal of Industrial Economics*, vol 32, pp. 435–450.

Cliff, T. (1970), *The Employers' Offensive*, London, Pluto Press.

Clower, R.W. (1965), 'The Keynesian counter-revolution: a theoretical appraisal', in F.H. Hahn and F. Brechling (eds), *The Theory of Interest Rates*, London, Macmillan.

Conyon, .M.J. (1988), An empirical investigation into income distribution, market structure and unionisation in UK manufacturing 1980–1984', University of Warwick, *Warwick Economic Research Paper*, no. 306 (November).

Costrell, R.M. (1981), 'Overhead labor and the cyclical behavior of productivity and real wages', *Journal of Post-Keynesian Economics*, vol. 3, pp. 277–290.

Council on Prices, Productivity and Profits (1961), *Fourth Report*, London, HMSO (July).

Coutts, K., Godley, W. and Nordhaus, W.D. (1978), *Industrial Pricing in the United Kingdom*, Cambridge, Cambridge University Press.

Cowling, K. (1982), *Monopoly Capitalism*, London, Macmillan.

Cowling, K. (1983), 'Excess capacity and the degree of collusion: oligopoly behaviour in the slump', *Manchester School*, vol. 53, pp. 341–359.

Cowling, K. (1985), 'Economic obstacles to democracy', in R.C.O. Matthews (ed.), *Economy and Democracy*, London, Macmillan.

Cowling, K. and Molho, I. (1982), 'Wage share, concentration and unionism', *Manchester School*, vol. 50, pp. 99–115.

Cowling, K. and Mueller, D.C. (1978), 'The social costs of monopoly power', *Economic Journal*, vol. 88, pp. 46–68.

Cowling, K. and Sugden, R. (1987), *Transnational Monopoly Capitalism*, Brighton, Wheatsheaf.

Cowling, K. and Waterson, M. (1976), 'Price–cost margins and market structure', *Economica*, vol. 43, pp. 267–74.

Craven, J. (1979), *The Distribution of the Product*, London, George Allen and Unwin.

Cross, R. (ed.) (1988), *Unemployment, Hysteresis and the Natural Rate Hypothesis*, Oxford, Blackwell.

Cubbin, J. and Leech, D. (1983), 'The effect of shareholding dispersion on the degree of control in British companies: theory and measurement', *Economic Journal*, vol. 93, pp. 351–369.

Curry, B. and George, K.C. (1983), 'Industrial concentration: a survey', *Journal of Industrial Economics*, vol. 31, pp.203–255.

Daniel, W.W. (1975), , *The PEP Survey on Inflation*, London, Political and Economic Planning Broadsheet.

Dean, J.W. (1981), 'The dissolution of the Keynesian consensus', in Bell, D. and Kristol, I. (eds), *The Crisis in Economic Theory*, New York, Basic Books.

Demsetz, H. (1973), 'Industrial structure, market rivalry and public policy', *Journal of Law and Economics*, vol. 16, pp. 1–9.

DeRosa, D. and Goldstein, M. (1982), 'The cross-sectional price equation: a comment', *American Economic Review*, vol. 72, pp. 976–983.

Disney, R. and Gospel, H. (1989), 'The seniority model of trade union behaviour: a (partial) defence', *British Journal of Industrial Relations*, vol. 27, pp. 179–195.

Dixit, A. (1976), *The Theory of Equilibrium Growth*, London, Oxford University Press.

Dixit, A. (1980), 'The role of investment in entry deterrence', *Economic Journal*, vol. 90, pp. 95–106.

Domar, E. (1946), 'Capital formation, rate of growth and unemployment', *Econometrica*, vol. 14, pp. 137–147.

Domberger, S. (1979), 'Price adjustment and market structure', *Economic Journal*, vol. 89, pp. 96–108.

Domberger, S. (1983), *Industrial Structure, Pricing and Inflation*, Oxford, Martin Robertson.

Domowitz, I., Hubbard, R.G. and Petersen, B.C. (1986a), 'Business cycles and the relationship between concentration and price–cost margins', *Rand Journal of Economics*, vol. 17, pp. 1–17.

Domowitz, I., Hubbard, R.G. and Petersen, B.C. (1986b), 'The inter-temporal stability of the concentration-margins relationship', *Journal of Industrial Economics*, vol. 35, pp. 13–34.

Domowitz, I., Hubbard, R.G. and Petersen, B.C. (1988), 'Market structure and cyclical fluctuations in U.S. manufacturing', *Review of Economics and Statistics*, vol. 70, pp. 55–66.

Donovan Commission (1968) (Royal Commission on Trades Unions and Employers Association), chairman: Lord Donovan, *Report*, London, HMSO (Cmnd 3623).

Downs, A. (1957), *An Economic Theory of Democracy*, New York, Harper and Row.

Dunlop, J.T. (1950), *Wage Determination under Trades Unions*, New York, Kelley.

Dutt, A.K. (1984), 'Stagnation, income distribution and monopoly power', *Cambridge Journal of Economics*, vol. 8, pp. 25–40.

Edwards, R. and Podgursky, M. (1986), 'The unravelling accord: American unions in crisis', pp. 14–60 in Edwards, R., Garonna, P. and Todtling, F., *Unions in Crisis and Beyond: Perspectives from Six Countries*, Dover MA, Auburn House Publishing.

Farber, H.S. (1978), 'Individual union preferences and union wage determination: the case of the United Mine Workers', *Journal of Political Economy*, vol. 86, pp. 923–942.

Feinstein, C.H. (1968), 'Changes in the distribution of the national income in the United Kingdom since 1860' in J. Marchal and B. Ducros (eds), *The Distribution of National Income*. London, Macmillan.

Feiwel, G. (1974), 'Reflection on Kalecki's theory of political business cycle', *Kyklos*, vol. 27, pp. 21–48.

Feiwel, G. (1975), *The Intellectual Capital of Michal Kalecki*,

Knoxville, University of Tennessee Press.

Feldstein, M. and Summers, L. (1977), 'Is the rate of profit falling?', *Brookings Papers on Economic Activity*. no. 1, pp. 211–227.

Ferguson, C.E. (1969), *The Neoclassical Theory of Production and Distribution*, Cambridge, Cambridge University Press.

Ferguson, P.R. (1988), *Industrial Economics: Issues and Perspectives*, London, Macmillan.

Fine, B. and Murfin, A. (1984), *Macroeconomics and Monopoly Capitalism*, Brighton, Wheatsheaf.

Fitzroy, F.R. and Kraft, K. (1985), 'Unionization, wages and efficiency: theories and evidence from the US and West Germany', *Kyklos*, vol. 38, pp. 537–554.

Foster, J.B. and Szlajfer, H. (eds) (1984), *The Faltering Economy: The Problem of Accumulation under Monopoly Capitalism*, New York, Monthly Review Press.

Frank, J. (1986), *The New Keynesian Economics*, Brighton, Wheatsheaf.

Freeman, R.B. (1976), 'Individual mobility and union voice in the labor market', *American Economic Review Papers and Proceedings*, vol. 66, pp. 135–141.

Freeman, R.B. and Medoff, J.L. (1979), 'New estimates of private sector unionism in the United States', *Industrial and Labor Relations Review*, vol. 32, pp. 143–174.

Freeman, R.B. and Medoff, J.L. (1983), 'Unionism, price–cost margins, and the return to capital', National Bureau of Economic Research, Discussion Paper No. 1164, Cambridge, MA (July).

Freeman, R.B. and Medoff, J.L. (1984), *What Do Unions Do?*, New York, Basic Books.

Frey, B.S. and Schneider, F. (1975), 'On the modelling of politico-economic interdependence', *European Journal of Political Research*, vol. 3, pp. 339–360.

Funke, M. (1986), 'Influences on the profitability of the manufacturing sector in the UK – an empirical study, *Oxford Bulletin of Economics and Statistics*, vol. 48, pp. 165–187.

Gaffikin, F. and Nickson, A. (1984), *Jobs Crisis and the Multinationals: Deindustrialisation in the West Midlands*, Birmingham, Third World Books.

Gallie, D. (1978), *In Search of the New Working Class: Automation and Social Integration within the Capitalist Enterprise*, Cambridge, Cambridge University Press.

Geroski, P.A. and Jacquemin, A. (1981), 'Imports as a competitive discipline', *Recherches Economiques de Louvain*, vol. 47, pp. 197–208.

Glyn, A. and Sutcliffe, R.B. (1972), *British Capitalism, Workers and the Profits Squeeze*, Harmondsworth, Penguin.

Godley, W.A.H. and Nordhaus, W.D. (1972), 'Pricing in the trade cycle', *Economic Journal*, vol. 89, pp. 96–108.

Gordon, M.J. (1985), 'The post-war growth in monopoly power', *Journal of Post-Keynesian Economics*, vol. 8, pp. 3–13.

Gorman, J. (1972), 'Nonfinancial corporations: new measures of input and output', *Survey of Current Business*, March.

Green, F. (1982), 'Occupational pension schemes and British capitalism', *Cambridge Journal of Economics*, vol. 6, pp. 267–283.

Hahn, F.H. (1973), *On the Notion of Equilibrium in Economics: An Inaugural Lecture*, Cambridge, Cambridge University Press.

Hahnel, R. and Sherman, H.J. (1982a), 'The rate of profit over the business cycle', *Cambridge Journal of Economics*, vol. 6, pp. 185–194.

Hahnel, R. and Sherman, H.J. (1982b), 'Income distribution and the business cycle: three conflicting hypotheses', *Journal of Economic Issues*, vol. 16, pp. 49–73.

Hall, R.E. (1986), 'Market structure and macroeconomic fluctuations', *Brookings Papers on Economic Activity*, no. 2, pp. 285–322.

Hannah, L. (1983), *The Rise of the Corporate Economy*, 2nd edn, London, Methuen.

Harcourt, G.C. (1972), *Some Cambridge Controversies in the Theory of Capital*, Cambridge, Cambridge University Press.

Hargreaves-Heap, S. (1980), 'World profitability crisis in the 1970's: some empirical evidence', *Capital and Class*, no. 12, pp. 66–84.

Hart, P.E. and Morgan, E. (1977), 'Market structure and economic performance in the UK', *Jourenal of Industrial Economics*, vol. 25, pp. 177–193.

Haskel, J. (1987), 'The updated CLE quarterly GB data set', Centre for Labour Economics, London School of Economics, *Working Paper*, No. 948.

Henley, A.G. (1986a), 'Wage share, market power and unionism: a reply to Brush and Crane', *Manchester School*, vol. 54, pp. 104–108.

Henley, A.G. (1986b), 'Empirical studies on the determination of the functional distribution of income', unpublished Doctoral thesis, University of Warwick (June).

Henley, A.G. (1987a), 'Trades unions, market concentration and income distribution in United States manufacturing industry', *International Journal of Industrial Organization*, vol. 5, pp. 193–210.

Henley, A.G. (1987b), 'Labour's shares and profitability crisis in the U.S.: recent experience and post-war trends', *Cambridge Journal of Economics*, vol. 11, pp. 315–330.

Henley, A.G. (1988a), 'Price formation and market structure: the case of the inter-war coal industry', *Oxford Bulletin of Economics and Statistics*, vol. 50, pp. 263–278.

Henley, A.G. (1988b), 'Political aspects of full employment: a reassessment of Kalecki', *The Political Quarterly*, vol. 59, pp. 437–450.

Henley, A.G. (1989), 'Aggregate profitability and income distribution in the UK corporate sector 1963–1985', *International Review of Applied Economics*, vol. 3, pp. 170–190.

Hicks, J.R. (1965), *Capital and Growth*, London, Oxford University Press.

Hirsch, B.T. and Addison, J.T. (1986), *The Economic Analysis of Unions: New Approaches and Evidence*, Boston, Allen and Unwin.

Hirsch, F. and Gordon, D. (1975), *Newspaper Money*, London, Hutchinson.

Hitiris, T. (1978), 'Effective protection and economic performance in UK manufacturing industry, 1963 and 1968', *Economic Journal*, vol. 88, pp. 107–120.

Howard, M.C. (1979), *Modern Theories of Income Distribution*, London, Macmillan.

Hughes, A. and Kumar, M.S. (1984a), 'Recent trends in aggregate concentration in the United Kingdom economy', *Cambridge Journal of Economics*, vol. 8, pp. 235–250.

Hughes, A. and Kumar, M.S. (1984b), 'Recent trends in aggregate concentration in the United Kingdom economy: revised estimates', *Cambridge Journal of Economics*, vol. 8. pp. 401-402.

Hunt, E.K. and Schwartz, J.G. (1972), *A Critique of Economic Theory*, Harmondsworth, Penguin.

Johnson, H.G. (1973), *The Theory of Income Distribution*, London, Gray-Mills.

Kaldor, N. (1955), 'Alternative theories of distribution', *Review of Economic Studies*, vol. 23, pp. 83–100.

Kaldor, N. (1966), 'Marginal productivity and macroeconomic theories of distribution', *Review of Economic Studies*, vol. 33, pp. 309–19.

Kalecki, M. (1938), 'The determinants of the distribution of national income', *Econometrica*, vol. 6, pp. 97–102.

Kalecki, M. (1939), *Essays in the Theory of Economic Fluctuations*, London, Allen and Unwin.

Kalecki, M. (1943), 'Political aspects of full employment', *The Political Quarterly*, vol. 14, pp. 322–331.

Kalecki, M. (1945), 'Full employment by stimulating private investment?', *Oxford Economic Papers*, no. 7, pp. 83–93.

Kalecki, M. (1954), *Theory of Economic Dynamics*, London, Allen and Unwin.

Kalecki, M. (1971a), *Selected Essays on the Dynamics of the Capitalist Economy 1933–1970*, Cambridge, Cambridge University Press.

Kalecki, M. (1971b), 'Class struggle and the distribution of income', *Kyklos*, vol. 24, pp. 1–9 (also reprinted as Chap. 14 of Kalecki, 1971a).

Kalecki, M. (1972), *The Last Phase in the Transformation of Capitalism*, New York, Monthly Review Press.

Kalleberg, A.L., Wallace, M. and Raffalovich, L.E. (1984), 'Accounting for labor's share: class and income distribution in the printing industry', *Industrial and Labor Relations Review*, vol. 37, pp. 386–402.

Karier, T. (1985), 'Unions and monopoly profits', *Review of Economics and Statistics*, vol. 67, pp. 34–42.

Karier, T. (1988), 'New evidence on the effect of unions and imports on monopoly power, *Journal of Post-Keynesian Economics*, vol. 10, 414–427.

Kennedy, C. and Thirlwall, A.P. (1973), 'Technical progress: a survey', *Economic Journal*, vol. 83, pp. 11–72.

Kerr, C. (1957), 'Labor's income share and the labor movement' in G.W. Taylor and F.C. Pierson (eds), *New Concepts in Wage Determination*, New York, McGraw-Hill.

Khalilzadeh-Shirazi, J. (1974), 'Market structure and price–cost margins in United Kingdom manufacturing industries', *Review of Economics and Statistics*, vol. 56, pp. 67–76.

Kilpatrick, A. and Lawson, T. (1980), 'On the nature of industrial decline in the UK', *Cambridge Journal of Economics*, 4, 85-102.

King, J.E. and Regan, P. (1976), *Relative Income Shares*, London, Macmillan.

King, M.A. (1975), 'The United Kingdom profits crisis: myth or reality?', *Economic Journal*, vol. 85, pp. 33–54.

Kochan, T.A., Katz, H.C. and McKersie, R.B. (1986), *The Transformation of American Industrial Relations*, New York, Basic Books.

Kotz, D. (1982), 'Monopoly, inflation and economic crisis', *Review of Radical Political Economics*, vol. 14, pp. 1–17.

Kravis, I. (1959), 'Relative income shares in fact and theory', *American Economic Review*, pp. 917–949.

Kravis, I. (1968), 'Income distribution: functional shares' in D.L. Sills (ed.), *International Journal of the Social Sciences*, New York, Macmillan and Free Press.

Kriesler, P. (1987), *Kalecki's Microanalysis*, Cambridge, Cambridge University Press.

Kriesler, P. (1988), 'Kalecki's pricing theory revisited', *Journal of Post-Keynesian Economics*, vol. 11, pp. 108–130.

Layard, P.R.G. and Nickell, S.J. (1985), 'The causes of British unemployment', *National Institute Economic Review*, no. 111, pp. 62–85.

Layard, P.R.G. and Nickell, S.J. (1986a), 'Unemployment in Britain', *Economica*, vol. 53 (supplement), pp. s121–s170.

Layard, P.R.G. and Nickell, S.J. (1986b), 'Data appendix to Unemployment in Britain', *Economica*, vol. 53, Supplement, pp. s368–s374.

Leech, D. (1987), 'Corporate ownership and control: a new look at the evidence of Berle and Means', *Oxford Economic Papers*, vol. 39, pp. 534–551.

Leijonhufvud, A. (1968), *On Keynesian Economics and the Economics of Keynes*, London, Oxford University Press.

Levhari, D.E. (1965), 'A non-substitution theorem and switching of techniques', *Quarterly Journal of Economics*, vol. 79, pp. 98–105.

Levinson, H.M. (1954), 'Collective bargaining and income distribution', *American Economic Review Papers and Proceedings*, vol. 44, pp. 308–316.

Lewis, H.G. (1983), 'Union relative wage effects: a survey of macro estimates', *Journal of Labor Economics*, vol. 1, pp. 1–27.

Lindbeck, A. and Snower, D. (1986), 'Wage setting, unemployment and insider–outsider relations', *American Economic Review Papers and Proceedings*, vol. 76, pp. 235–239.

Littlechild, S.C. (1981), 'Misleading calculations of the social costs of monopoly power', *Economic Journal*, vol. 91, pp. 348–363.

Locksley, G. (1978), 'Trades unions and unemployment', *Political Quarterly*, vol. 49, pp. 483–489.

Locksley, G. (1980), 'The political business cycle: alternative interpretations', in P. Whiteley (ed.), *Model of Political Economy*, London, Sage Publications.

Lustgarten, S. (1975), *Industrial Concentration and Inflation*, Washington D.D., American Enterprise Institute for Public Policy Research.

Lyons, B. (1986), 'The welfare loss due to strategic investment in excess capacity', *International Journal of Industrial Organisation*, vol. 4, pp. 109–120.

Machin, S.J. (1988a), 'The productivity effects of unionisation and firm size in British engineering firms', *Warwick Economic Research Paper*, no. 293, University of Warwick (March).

Machin, S.J. (1988b), 'Unions and the capture of economic rents: an investigation using British firm level data', Discussion Paper no. 89-02, Department of Economics, University College, London (October).

Macrae, D.C. (1977), 'A political model of the business cycle', *Journal of Political Economy*, vol. 85, pp. 239–263.

Maddala, G.S. (1988), *Introduction to Econometrics*, New York, Macmillan.

Manning, A. (1987), 'Trade union power and jobs: theory and policy', *International Review of Applied Economics*, vol. 1, pp. 176–189.

Marginson, P. (1985), 'The multidivisional firm and control over the work process', *International Journal of Industrial Organization*, vol 3, pp. 37–56.

Martin, W.E. (ed.) (1978), *The Economics of the Profits Crisis*, London, HMSO.

Masson, R.T. and Shaanan, J. (1986), 'Excess capacity and limit pricing: an empirical test', *Economica*, vol. 53, pp. 365–378.

McDonald, I.M. (1985), 'Market power and unemployment', *International Journal of Industrial Organization*, vol. 3, pp. 21–36.

McKersie, R. and Hunter, L. (1973), *Pay, Productivity and Collective Bargaining*, London, Macmillan.

Meade, J. (1986), *Alternative Systems of Business Organization and of Workers' Remuneration*, London, Allen and Unwin.

Mendis, L. and Muellbauer, J. (1983), 'Has there been a British productivity breakthrough? evidence from an aggregate production function for manufacturing', *London School of Economics Centre for Labour Economics*, Discussion Paper no. 170.

Metwally, M. and Tamaschke, H. (1981), 'Advertising and the propensity to consume', *Oxford Bulletin of Economics and Statistics*, vol. 43, pp. 273–286.

Michl, T.R. (1989), 'The two stage decline in the U.S. nonfinancial corporate profitability, 1948-1986', *Review of Radical Political Economics* (forthcoming).

Minford, A.P.L. (1983), 'Labour market equilibrium in an open economy', *Oxford Economic Papers*, vol. 35 (supplement), pp. 207–244.

Minns, R. (1980), *Pension Funds and British Capitalism*, London, Heinemann.

Mitchell, D. (1985), 'Shifting norms in wage determination', *Brookings Papers on Economic Activity*, no. 2, pp. 575–599.

Mitchell, W. (1951), *What Happens During Business Cycles*, New York, National Bureau of Economic Research.

Moroney, J.R. and Allen, B.T. (1969), 'Monopoly power and the relative share of labor', *Industrial and Labor Relations Review*, vol. 22, pp. 167–178.

Moseley, F. (1985), 'The rate of surplus value in the post-war U.S. economy: a critique of Weisskopf's estimates', *Cambridge Journal of Economics*, vol. 9, pp. 57–79.

Mueller, W.F. and Hamm, L.G. (1974), 'Trends in industrial concentration 1947 to 1970', *Review of Economics and Statistics*, vol. 56, pp. 511–520.

Mulvey, C. (1976), 'Collective agreements and relative earnings in UK manufacturing in 1973', *Economica*, vol. 43, pp. 419–427.

Munley, F. (1981), 'Wages, salaries and the profit share: a reassessment of the evidence', *Cambridge Journal of Economics*, vol. 5, pp. 159–173.

Nell, E. (1988), *Prosperity and Public Spending*, London, Unwin Hyman.

Nerlove, M. (1967), 'Recent empirical studies of the C.E.S. and related production functions', in Murray Brown (ed) *The Theory and Empirical Analysis of Production*, New York, National Bureau of Economic Research, pp. 55–122.

Nickell, S.J. (1982), 'A bargaining model of the Philips Curve', London School of Economics, Centre for Labour Economics *Discussion Paper* No. 130.

Nordhaus, W.D. (1974), 'The falling share of profits', *Brookings Papers on Economic Activity*, no. 1, pp. 169–208.

Nordhaus, W.D. (1975), 'The political business cycle', *Review of Economic Studies*, vol. 42, pp. 160–190.

Ornstein, S.I. (1977), *Industrial Concentration and Advertising Intensity*, Washington D.C., American Enterprise Institute for Public Policy Research.

Oswald, A.J. (1984), 'Efficient contracts are on the labour demand curve: theory and facts', Princeton University, Industrial Relations Section, Working Paper no. 178, July.

Oswald, A.J. (1985), 'The economic theory of trades unions: an introductory survey', *Scandinavian Journal of Economics*, vol. 87, pp. 197–233.

Oswald, A.J. and Turnbull, P.J. (1985), 'Pay and employment determination in Britain: what are labour contracts really like?', *Oxford Review of Economic Policy*, vol. 1, pp. 80–97.

Panic, M. and Close, R.E. (1973), 'Profitability of British manufacturing industry', *Lloyds Bank Review*, July.

Parsley, C.J. (1980), 'Labor union effects on wage gains: a survey of recent literature', *Journal of Economic Literature*, vol. 18, pp. 1–31.

Pasinetti, L.L. (1962), 'Rate of profit and income distribution in relation to the rate of economic growth', *Review of Economic Studies*, vol. 29, pp. 267–279.

Pasinetti, L.L. (1974), *Growth and Income Distribution: Essays in Economic Theory*, Cambridge, Cambridge University Press.

Peel, D. (1975), 'Advertising and aggregate consumption', in K. Cowling et al. (eds), *Advertising and Economic Behaviour*, London, Macmillan.

Perry, G.L. (1980), 'Inflation in theory and practice', *Brookings Papers on Economic Activity*, no. 1, pp. 207–241.

Phelps-Brown, E.H. (1983), *The Origins of Trade Union Power*, Oxford, Clarendon Press.

Phelps-Brown, E.H. and Hart, P.E. (1952), 'The share of wages in national income', *Economic Journal*, vol. 62, pp. 253–277.

Phillips, A.W. (1958), 'The relation between unemployment and the ratè of change of money wage rates in the United Kingdom, 1861–1957', *Economica*, vol. 38, pp. 283–299.

Piore, M. and Sabel, C. (1984), *The Second Industrial Divide*, New York, Basic Books.

Pitelis, C.N. (1987), *Corporate Capital: Control, Ownership, Saving and Crisis*, Cambridge, Cambridge University Press.

Pitelis, C.N. and Sugden, R. (1986), 'The separation of ownership and control in the theory of the firm: a reappraisal', *International Journal of Industrial Organization*, vol. 4, pp. 69–86.

Posner, R.A. (1975), 'The social costs of monopoly and regulation', *Journal of Political Economy*, vol. 83, pp. 807–827.

Prais, S.J. (1976), *The Evolution of Giant Firms in Britain*, Cambridge, Cambridge University Press.

Reder, M. (1959), 'Alternative theories of labor's share', in M.

Abramovitz et al. (eds) *The Allocation of Economic Resources: Essays in Honour of B.F. Haley*, Stanford, Stanford University Press.

Reekie, W.D. (1979), *Industries, Prices and Markets*, Oxford, Phillip Allan.

Reynolds, P.J. (1983), 'Kalecki's degree of monopoly', *Journal of Post-Keynesian Economics*, vol. 5, pp. 493–503.

Reynolds, P.J. (1984), 'An empirical analysis of the degree of monopoly theory of distribution', *Bulletin of Economic Research*, vol. 36, pp. 59–84.

Reynolds, P.J. (1987), *Political Economy: A Synthesis of Kaleckian and Post Keynesian Economics*, Brighton, Wheatsheaf.

Riach, R. (1971), 'Kalecki's "Degree of Monopoly" reconsidered', *Australian Economic Papers*, vol. 10, pp. 50–60.

Ripley, F.C. and Segal, L. (1973), 'Price determination in 395 manufacturing industries', *Review of Economics and Statistics*, vol. 60, pp. 263–271.

Robinson, J. (1933), *The Economics of Imperfect Competition*, London, Macmillan.

Robinson, J. (1960), 'The theory of distribution' in *Collected Economic Papers, Volume 2*, Oxford, Basil Blackwell.

Ross, A.M. (1948), *Trade Union Wage Policy*, Berkeley, University of California Press.

Rotemberg, J.J. (1982), 'Sticky prices in the United States', *Journal of Political Economy*, vol. 90, pp. 1187–1211.

Rotemberg, J.J. and Saloner, G. (1986), 'A supergame theoretic model of price-wars during booms', *American Economic Review*, vol. 76, pp. 390–407.

Rowthorn, R. (1977), 'Conflict, inflation and money', *Cambridge Journal of Economics*, vol. 1, pp. 215–239 reprinted in Rowthorn, R., *Capitalism, Conflict and Inflation*, London Lawrence and Wishart, 1980.

Rowthorn, R. (1981), 'Demand, real wages, and economic growth', *Thames Papers in Political Economy*, Thames Polytechnic (Autumn).

Salinger, M.A. (1984), 'Tobin's q, unionization and the concentration–profits relationship', *Rand Journal of Economics*, vol. 15, pp. 159–170.

Samuelson, P.A. (1962), 'Parable and realism in capital theory: the surrogate production function', *Review of Economic Studies*, vol. 39, pp. 193–206.

Sawyer, M.C. (1980), 'Monopoly welfare loss in the United Kingdom', *Manchester School*, vol. 50, pp. 331–354.

Sawyer, M.C. (1982a), *Macroeconomics in Question: The Keynesian Monetarist Orthodoxies and the Kaleckian Alternative*, Brighton, Wheatsheaf.

Sawyer, M.C. (1982b), 'Collective bargaining, oligopoly, and macro-economics', *Oxford Economic Papers*, vol. 34, pp. 428–448.

Sawyer, M.C. (1983), *Business Pricing and Inflation*, London, Macmillan.

Sawyer, M.C. (1985a), *The Economics of Michal Kalecki*, London, Macmillan.

Sawyer, M.C. (1985b), *The Economics of Industries and Firms*, 2nd edn, London, Croom Helm.

Sawyer, M.C. (1988), 'Theories of monopoly capitalism', *Journal of Economic Surveys*, vol. 2, pp. 47–76.

Scherer, F.M. (1980), *Industrial Market Structure and Economic Performance*, 2nd edn, Boston, Houghton Mifflin.

Schultze, C. (1975), 'Falling profits, rising profit margins, and the full employment profit rate', *Brookings Papers on Economic Activity*, no. 2, pp. 449–469.

Shah, A. (1984), 'Job attributes and the size of the union/non-union wage differential', *Economica*, vol. 51, pp. 437–446.

Shepherd, W.G. (1982), 'Causes of increased competition in the U.S. economy 1939–1980', *Review of Economics and Statistics*, vol. 64, pp. 613–626.

Sherman, H.J. (1986), *Profits in the United States: An Introduction to a Study of Economic Concentration and Business Cycles*, New York, Cornell University Press.

Sherman, H.J. (1977), 'Monopoly power and stagflation', *Review of Radical Political Economics*, vol. 11, pp. 269–284.

Sherman, H.J. (1986), 'Changes in the character of the U.S. business cycle', *Review of Radical Political Economics*, vol. 18, pp. 190–204.

Sherman, H.J. (1987), 'The business cycle of capitalism', *International Review of Applied Economics*, vol. 1, pp. 72–85.

Simler, N.J. (1961), 'Unionism and labor's share in manufacturing industries', *Review of Economics and Statistics*, vol. 43, pp. 369–78.

Skidelsky, R. (ed.) (1977), *The End of the Keynesian Era*, London, Macmillan.

Smiley, R. (1988), 'Empirical evidence on strategic entry deterrence', *International Journal of Industrial Organization*, vol. 6, pp. 167–180.

Smith, D. (1987), *The Rise and Fall of Monetarism*, Harmondsworth, Penguin.

Solow, R.M. (1957), 'Technical change and the aggregate production function', *Review of Economics and Statistics*, vol. 39, pp. 312–20.

Solow, R.M. (1970), *Growth Theory: An Exposition*, Oxford, Oxford University Press.

Solow, R.M. (1985), 'Insiders and outsiders in wage determination', *Scandinavian Journal of Economics*, vol. 87, pp. 411–428.

Spence, A.M. (1977), 'Entry capacity, investment and oligopolistic pricing', *Bell Journal of Economics*, vol. 8, pp. 534–544.

Sraffa, P. (1960), *Production of Commodities by Means of Commodities*, Cambridge, Cambridge University Press.

Steindl, J. (1952), *Maturity and Stagnation in American Capitalism*, Oxford, Basil Blackwell (reprinted by Monthly Review Press, New York, 1976).

Steindl, J. (1979), 'Stagnation theory and stagnation policy', *Cambridge Journal of Economics*, vol. 3, pp. 1–14.

Stewart, M.B. (1983), 'Relative earnings and individual union membership in the United Kingdom', *Economica*, vol. 60, pp. 111–125.

Sugden, R. (1983), 'The degree of monopoly, international trade, and transnational corporations', *International Journal of Industrial Organisation*, vol. 1, pp. 165–187.

Sweezy, P.M. (1939), 'Demand under conditions of oligopoly', *Journal of Political Economy*, vol. 47, pp. 568–573.

Taylor, L. (1983), *Structuralist Macroeconomics*, New York, Basic Books.

Taylor, L. (1985), 'A stagnationist model of economic growth', *Cambridge Journal of Economics*, vol. 9, pp. 383–404.

Taylor, L.D. and Weiserbs, D. (1972), 'Advertising and the aggregate consumption function', *American Economic Review*, vol. 62, pp. 642–655.

Terry, M. (1977), "The inevitable growth of informality', *British Journal of Industrial Relations*, vol. 15, pp. 76–90.

Thurow, L.C. (1976), *Generating Inequality*, London, Macmillan.

Tinbergen, J. (1952), *On the Theory of Economic Policy*, Amsterdam, North-Holland.

Turnbull, P.J. (1988a), 'Industrial relations and the seniority model of union behaviour', *Oxford Bulletin of Economics and Statistics*, vol. 50, pp. 53–70.

Turnbull, P.J. (1988b), 'The economic theory of trade union behaviour: a critique', *British Journal of Industrial Relations*, vol. 26, pp. 99–118.

Union of Radical Political Economists (1978), *U.S. Capitalism in Crisis*, New York.

Voos, P.B. and Mischel, L.R. (1986), 'The union impact on profits: evidence from industry price–cost margin data', *Journal of Labor Economics*, vol. 4, pp. 105–33.

Wadhwani, S. and Wall, M. (1986), 'The UK capital stock – new estimates of premature scrapping', *Oxford Review of Economic Policy*, vol. 2, pp. 44–55.

Wagner, R.E. (1977), 'Economic manipulation for political profit: macroeconomic consequences and constitutional implication', *Kyklos*, vol. 30, pp. 394–410.

Waterson, M. (1984), *Economic Theory of the Industry*, Cambridge University Press.

Weiss, L.W. (1974), 'The concentration–profits relationship and anti-trust', in H.J. Goldschmid et al. (eds), *Industrial Concentration: The New Learning*, Boston, Little Brown.

Weiss, L.W. and Pascoe, G. (1981), 'Adjusted concentration ratios in manufacturing –1972', *mimeo*, Federal Trade Commission, Washington D.C.

Weisskopf, T.E. (1979), 'Marxian crisis theory and the rate of profit in the post-war U.S. economy', *Cambridge Journal of Economics*, vol. 3, pp. 341–378.

Weisskopf, T.E. (1981), 'Wages, salaries and profit share: a rejoinder', *Cambridge Journal of Economics*, vol. 5, pp. 175–182.

Weitzman, M. (1983), 'Some macroeconomic implications of alternative compensation systems', *Economic Journal*, vol. 93, pp. 763–783.

Weitzman, M. (1984), *The Share Economy*, Cambridge MA, Harvard University Press.

White, H. (1980), 'A heteroskedasticity-consistent covariance matrix estimator and a direct test for heteroskedasticity', *Econometrica*, vol. 48, pp. 817–838.

White, L.J. (1981), 'What has been happening to aggregate concentration in the United States?', *Journal of Industrial Economics*, vol. 29, pp. 223–230.

Wilder, R.P., Williams, G.W. and Singh, D. (1977), 'The price equation: a cross sectional approach', *American Economic Review*, vol. 67, pp. 732–740.

Wolff, E.N. (1986), 'The productivity slowdown and the fall in the US rate of profit, 1947–1976', *Review of Radical Political Economics*, vol. 18, pp. 87–109.

Zeitlin, M. (1974), 'Corporate ownership and control: the large corporation and the capitalist class', *American Journal of Sociology*, vol. 79, no. 5, pp. 1073–1119.

Author Index

Subject Index